Self Sabotage

How to Overcome Obstacles and Achieve Lasting Success

(Begin to Experience Mindfully the Life You Deserve)

James Yazzie

Published By **Cathy Nedrow**

James Yazzie

All Rights Reserved

Self Sabotage: How to Overcome Obstacles and Achieve Lasting Success (Begin to Experience Mindfully the Life You Deserve)

ISBN 978-1-9991564-3-5

No part of this guidebook shall be reproduced in any form without permission in writing from the publisher except in the case of brief quotations embodied in critical articles or reviews.

Legal & Disclaimer

The information contained in this book is not designed to replace or take the place of any form of medicine or professional medical advice. The information in this book has been provided for educational & entertainment purposes only.

The information contained in this book has been compiled from sources deemed reliable, and it is accurate to the best of the Author's knowledge; however, the Author cannot guarantee its accuracy and validity and cannot be held liable for any errors or omissions. Changes are periodically made to this book. You must consult your doctor or get professional medical advice before using any of the suggested remedies, techniques, or information in this book.

Upon using the information contained in this book, you agree to hold harmless the Author from and against any damages, costs, and expenses, including any legal fees potentially resulting from the application of any of the information provided by this guide. This disclaimer applies to any damages or injury caused by the use and application, whether directly or indirectly, of any advice or information presented, whether for breach of contract, tort, negligence, personal injury, criminal intent, or under any other cause of action.

You agree to accept all risks of using the information presented inside this book. You need to consult a professional medical practitioner in order to ensure you are both able and healthy enough to participate in this program.

Table Of Contents

Chapter 1: Recognizing the Enemy Within

There is a vital 2nd that masses of us revel in within the region of self-discovery—the time even as we in the end meet the mysterious foe who has been silently retaining us decrease back: the enemy inner. This consciousness is not only a theoretical idea; it is a memorable enjoy for humans who've traveled the tough direction of self-development. When I was at a crossroads among my goals and insecurities, this interest hit me like a bolt of lightning. The complicated internet of self-sabotage I had by way of accident created spherical myself changed into as although a curtain were pulled, exposing it. S

I had cautiously masked truths in self-deception; however know-how the enemy inner determined them. A flood of recollections got here flooding yet again as I have become inward: times as soon as I hesitated out of self-doubt; instances as soon as I clung to the safety of my acquainted surroundings; times on the same time as worry controlled my movements. Realizing I had regularly set my personal limitations changed into terrifying.

This awakening wasn't without its percent of emotions. I actually have end up angry because I found out how masses I were impeding my very very own improvement. There modified right into a enjoy of urgency as well, a burning choice to tear down the ones obstacles I had mounted my very personal way and ultimately strengthen without catch 22 situation. Being the protagonist and the antagonist of 1's private tale at the identical time is a peculiar feeling.

The adversary internal isn't always a unmarried element; as an opportunity, it is the stop give up result of a fixed of cumulative thoughts, research, and perceptions through time. It's the ominous echoes of vintage criticisms, the hesitancies delivered on by the usage of disasters, and the sneaky whispers that puzzled my well really worth. In order to defeat this adversary, I had to be organized to test each hassle of my personal psychology and find out the deliver of my fears. It turned into a challenge that required vulnerability—accepting the uncomfortability of admitting to scars that had in no manner clearly healed.

This warfare modified into no longer an remoted one. A aid tool commenced to form, which consist of buddies, mentors, or maybe authors whose writing served as a beacon for the duration of the maze of self-discovery. I started a journey of self-interest with their assist. I started practising mindfulness, discovering the triggers that would ship me sliding into self-doubt and studying to word my mind with out passing judgment. Learning that I had the capability to change the tale of my mind grow to be each liberating and difficult.

During this ongoing quest, I placed the exercise of self-compassion, that could be a salve for the accidents because of years of self-complaint. I positioned out to expose myself the same compassion and expertise that I freely gave to others, instead of criticizing myself for perceived flaws. I become capable of view my losses as stepping stones and each failure as a lesson in preference to a condemnation through viewing them thru a compassionate lens.

Recognizing the inner enemy, however, changed into handiest step one. It was a recognition that opened the door for transformation, however it also referred to as for ongoing willpower to self-mastery. I realized that I had to be constantly aware of my mind, deeds, and selections if I preferred to defeat this foe. As I constantly puzzled the cozy narratives I had grown acquainted with, the manner in advance end up characterised with the useful resource of pain.

The potential to face and vanquish internal demons is established through this voyage, which demonstrates the depth of human perseverance. The fight towards the internal enemy is not a story of short victory however taken into consideration one of staying power, improvement, and self-discovery. This enemy's identity, earned via person battles and the enjoy of infinite others, is a transformative turning factor—a crucial junction wherein we begin to tear down the barricades we've got were given spent a lifetime erecting. With newly acquired self-hobby and a steadfast remedy to understand the whole ability that is inside us, we are invited to set out on this journey.

Understanding Self-Sabotage Cycle

I commenced a quest in the silent recesses of my mind to make revel in of the tangled net of feelings and moves that had imprisoned me for goodbye. A want for self-know-how and a burning preference to understand why I always regarded to get inside the manner of my personal fulfillment drove me on my revel in. A pattern started out out to show up as I descended greater into the depths of my mind—a cycle of self-destruction that had woven its threads into the very cloth of my life.

It became a cycle that often commenced with the harmless spark of a new undertaking or goal. My head may be swimming with opportunities, and my coronary coronary coronary heart may be racing with exhilaration. However, a quiet undercurrent of uncertainty may also creep in due to the fact the preliminary excitement subsided. The as speedy as-easy course within the the the front of me have end up obscured with the beneficial resource of fears and insecurities, casting doubt on the sunshine of my goals. The cycle began out out to take maintain at some stage in the ones exposed times.

It seemed that self-sabotage thrived on comfort. I permit the ones doubts grow, and that they ultimately have end up a chorus of condemnation of myself that rang frequently interior of me. I would begin to 2nd-bet my selections, question my abilties, and ultimately again a long way from the challenges that I had as quick as been so prepared to address. The perception in my capacity that I once had modified into erased, as if a quiet saboteur had moved into my head and feature end up whispering untruths that undermined my self-self notion.

With each era, the cycle have become increasingly more effective. I became greater glad that I wasn't deserving of success the more I allow self-doubt have an impact on my behavior. My worry of failing introduced on me to engage in behaviors that raised the opportunity of failing, which in turn established the concern. As a end end result, it became a self-beautiful prophecy. It turn out to be a vicious circle that kept me mired in a loop of defeat. It end up a brutal dance.

I had in no manner ventured to interact in the degree of reflected photo vital to interrupt loose from this loop. It known as for dropping mild on the darkish corners and addressing the whispered lies. It entailed accepting vulnerability and figuring out that self-sabotage wasn't a demonstration of inborn frailty however instead a coping method developed due to past traumas and insecurities.

I began to reveal the layers that had built over the years with the help of introspective techniques like journaling and mindfulness. I end up able to select out the triggers for my self-negative behavior with the resource of going again to instances at the identical time as my vulnerability have been met with harm. I end up able to decrease their have an impact on through figuring out the memories that had grown into a complex community of triggers that started the cycle.

However, comprehending the self-sabotage cycle have end up more than most effective a way to observe the preceding hurts; it turn out to be a call to movement. I started out to increase a contemporary courting with myself after turning into aware about this. Recognizing that I have become not the high-quality person going through this problem, I switched out self-complaint for self-compassion. I evolved the potential to confront the presumptions that had prolonged held me all over again and to doubt the veracity of my horrible thoughts.

It have emerge as a slow machine that called for staying power and tenacity. There were disasters, times while my solve became beaten through self-doubt's nagging voice. But after each setback, I have been given returned up with renewed strength and vowed to stop the cycle. I started out out out to replace vintage conduct with new ones, making affirmations to counteract negativity and taking measures to triumph over worry. Rewriting the story that had too prolonged guided my picks become a aware attempt on my detail.

A change occurred because of the reality the instances advanced into weeks and then into months. My lifelong companion, the cycle of self-negative conduct, commenced to permit cross. Instead, a experience of empowerment—a firmly held conviction that I may want to control my private destiny—emerged. Although the cycle remains gift, its have an effect on has lessened as self-focus and self-love come to be greater regular.

The first step on a lifelong adventure of improvement and recovery, information the self-sabotage cycle have grow to be no longer a panacea. It served as a reminder that I was on pinnacle of factors of writing my personal narrative and that I had the private freedom to conquer any constraints I had placed on myself. I continued to defy the cycle via making decisions that have been constant with my actual capacity, getting a touch bit toward the self-mastery I had extended desired.

Identifying Patterns of Self-Sabotage

Discovering the complex webs of self-sabotage is like decoding a mysterious map that leads us via the maze of our very own moves and alternatives in the labyrinth of private development. It became like peeling decrease back the layers of an onion as I set out on this undertaking to find out the self-damaging patterns woven into the cloth of my life; every revelation brought with it a combination of astonishment and comprehension. The way required me to have interaction in a peculiar introspection and function the braveness to face tough truths that had subtly customary my options for years.

Finding self-damaging dispositions required a journey into my preceding experiences in preference to into the unknown. A sample started to take form, one that related those reputedly unrelated incidents with a not unusual thread of self-defeat. It appeared with each case wherein my dreams seemed to stagnate, wherein my tries failed, or in which I come to be stuck in regular cycles of self-doubt. It have become a revelation that required me to be quite detached from my existence as a way to look the repeated patterns that avoided me from transferring beforehand.

This challenge exposed an internet of conduct that have supported self-sabotage. For instance, procrastination have come to be a trusted pal who frequently distracted me from my objectives. I might be drawn far from vital sports through manner of the attraction of immediately consolation, leaving a route of undone paintings in its wake. By delaying the project, I ought to justify a ability failure because of the fact the result of not having enough time rather than a lack of capability. Uncovering this dependancy pressured me to face the underlying fear of failure.

The exercising of poor self-talk, an inner monologue that had eroded my confidence through the years, have grow to be each different interwoven thread. The subliminal dependancy of downplaying my accomplishments, doubting my capabilities, and visualizing the worst-case conditions had served as a self-enjoyable prophecy, influencing my conduct to comply to the ones constraints that I had positioned on myself. This tendency, I positioned, had been cultivated thru preceding judgments and comparisons, demonstrating how profoundly out of doors impacts had permeated my head.

Understanding those styles required compassionate interest and an research of the crucial reasons of my self-destructive movements. It changed into a technique of reflected image that frequently pressured me to stand the uncomfortable reality that those physical games were a shape of protection—a way to guard myself from the possibility of unhappiness or rejection. Even though it regarded paradoxical, the inspiration of these self-unfavorable movements turn out to be a defective attempt to defend my mental properly-being.

The method of sample detection involved a dance between introspection and revelation in addition to eventual self-illumination. Resilience end up crucial for the transformational way because it required me to be inclined to deal with the ache of admitting my element in maintaining those conduct. But this recognition additionally brought strength. Now that I come to be privy to the ones tendencies, I modified into able to save you the instinctive reactions that had in advance precipitated my conduct.

There had been problems alongside the way. It took diligence and strive to overcome the ones styles' gravitational appeal. It involved rewiring my thoughts and laying down new neural pathways that led me a long way from my everyday self-sabotage detours. When I commenced out to fall lower returned into those vintage conduct, mindfulness helped me save you and gave me the space to make decisions that had been in keeping with my real dreams. It have come to be my compass.

In the cease, seeing self-damaging styles have become an research into my private humanity—a voyage that shed moderate at the subtle techniques we restriction our capability and the complexity of strength and fear. It became evidence of the complexity of private progress, in which the traumatic conditions we're dealing with are without a doubt as important as our victories. I set forth with newfound strength, a navigator with the talents to rewrite the story of my lifestyles one sample at a time, armed with the revelations obtained from my voyage.

Chapter 2: The Power of Self-Awareness

The profound pressure of self-popularity, which has the strength to trade the contours of our lives, is at the center of personal transformation. Genuine boom is constructed on this elusive however transformational electricity, which serves as the foundation. The workout of looking inward and putting off the outer layers of our thoughts, emotions, and motivations to locate our real selves is referred to as self-hobby. It's a method that encourages us to step out of doors of our recurring reactions and begin looking ourselves. We embark on a voyage of profound self-discovery whilst we encompass self-interest, one that famous the patterns that direct our moves, the convictions that have an effect on our perceptions, and the scars that impact our responses.

Beyond easy self-commentary, this ability is a device that lets in us to recognize our complete capability. We increase the capability to distinguish among impulses brought on by using the use of our real selves and people brought on with the aid of conditioning, societal expectancies, or unresolved feelings via self-reputation. It's a knowledge that permits us to choose responses which might be normal with our values and dreams with the useful resource of giving us the selection to pause earlier than reacting swiftly.

The capability of self-focus to break down the walls setting aside us from our real selves is what gives it its energy. We begin to get to the bottom of the complex internet of self-deception as we learn how to take note of our mind and emotions. We assignment the memories that have stored us in check and disprove the myths which have stunted our improvement. This approach is probably hard as it calls for bravery, vulnerability, and a readiness to actually accept pain to face the shadows interior. On the opportunity hand, it is on this suffering that we find out freedom. By being aware of our biases, problems, and insecurities, we are able to lessen their affect over us and go away them helpless in the face of aware attention.

Self-consciousness moreover serves as a stimulus for growing more potent relationships with others. We develop extra empathy and sensitivity to the feelings of others spherical us as we explore the terrain of our very own emotions. By bridging the space among humans, this empathic resonance promotes sincere connections primarily based mostly on compassion and records. Understanding our personal motivations permits us to higher realize others' intentions and harm thru preconceived notions and judgmental obstacles.

Developing self-recognition is an act of regaining our sovereignty on this age of instantaneous distractions and ordinary conversation. It grounds us in our internal compass the diverse noise of outside forces. It offers solace from the by no means-finishing need for approval from others through reminding us that our fee is defined through way of our alignment with our actual selves.

But self-attention is a way that requires endurance and willpower; it isn't always a holiday spot. It's a dependancy that develops as we keep to delve in addition into the mysterious depths of our psyche. Gentle but unyielding interest—the willingness to discover the depths of who we're with out bias or hurry—is what defines this revel in.

The capacity to be privy to oneself is largely an invitation to take once more manipulate of our lives. It lets in us to transport beyond the automated mode that regularly directs our conduct and gives us the strength to deliberately format our tale. It embodies honesty, demonstrates our capability for development, and honors the complexity of the human experience. As we start this experience within, we studies that the capability to be self-aware is not simply a device however moreover a lantern that leads us through the maze of our private existence and illuminates the manner to self-discovery, trade, and the fulfillment of our most functionality.

Cultivating Mindfulness for Self-Mastery

The voyage of profound self-discovery this is the exercise of mindfulness for self-mastery takes location inside the gift and has the energy to exchange the very fabric of our existence. The exercising of mindfulness consists of focusing our interest on the prevailing second at the equal time as letting move of our racing thoughts and turbulent emotional currents. In the midst of the craziness of present day existence, it offers a haven of clarity and peace with the resource of inviting us to observe our thoughts, sensations, and environment without passing judgment.

Through mindfulness, we make bigger the capability to phrase our very own tales at the same time as certainly acknowledging our mind and emotions. It's a way that teaches us to clearly take transport of every the immoderate fine and horrible additives of ourselves at the same time as destroying the automated behaviors of avoidance or denial that stifle our personal improvement. The undercurrents of our mind—the worries that maintain us decrease lower back, the aspirations that push us in advance, and the brief moments of tranquility that frequently slip our hobby—grow to be more apparent at the same time as we domesticate this nonjudgmental recognition.

The path to self-mastery begins with the cultivation of mindfulness, as it is thru this exercise that we benefit information of the complex workings of our minds. We come to apprehend that we are not described thru using our ideas as we watch them rise and fall like ocean waves. Instead, we're silent observers in their ebb and waft. This belief is transformational as it frees us from the control of our thoughts and lets in us to planned approximately our reactions in choice to performing on impulse.

Through meditation, breath reputation, body scans, or absolutely being definitely located in our each day sports, the journey of mindfulness can take many one in all a type bureaucracy. By regularly the use of the ones strategies, we hone our functionality to pay interest, extend our present-2d attention, and accumulate a profound experience of internal serenity. This inner calmness develops right into a deliver of fortitude that aids in guiding us thru life's storms with grace and poise.

Mindfulness is a key to more self-attention, emotional manipulate, and a stronger connection to our instinct within the international of self-mastery. It fosters tolerance and reputation, permitting us to tolerate the problems in each ourselves and the surroundings. By supporting us live anchored inside the present, this workout teaches us to permit pass of the weight of our beyond regrets and the tension we revel in approximately the destiny.

A profound relationship with our very personal thoughts, emotions, and reviews additionally may be evolved thru mindfulness. This in-intensity meditated photo famous the roots of ingrained behaviors and accidental patterns, beginning the door to planned trade. We can understand the idea styles that reason self-sabotage and frequently update them with movements that help our desires by the use of being attentive to those patterns.

As we amplify our mindfulness, we find out that self-mastery is a journey of release in preference to manipulate. It entails liberating ourselves from the manage of instinctive responses, the preserve of antique traumas, and the illusions which have imprisoned us. We come to understand that self-mastery is a lifelong journey that welcomes the now, transforms the past, and creates a future of authenticity, intentionality, and unrivaled self-awareness through the gentle exercise of mindfulness.

Unmasking Hidden Self-Sabotage Triggers

Identifying Covert Self-Sabotage Peeling back the layers of our unconscious mind to show the subtle and often mysterious reasons that inspire our self-defeating behavior is a manner referred to as triggers. These triggers characteristic as invisible strings that, while pulled, motive a chain of poor thoughts, feelings, and behaviors that preclude our development and nicely being. They frequently have their roots in in advance sports activities, traumas, or unexplored beliefs which have grow to be ingrained in our brains and feature an impact on our alternatives with out our aware cognizance. By starting the method of uncovering those triggers, we disclose the unseen forces which have sustained our self-sabotage, allowing us to neutralize them and reclaim manipulate over our selections and results.

We find out the complicated hyperlinks among outdoor stimuli and our indoors reactions through this research technique.

These triggers may additionally take the shape of reputedly unimportant events or feedback that unpredictably arouse emotions of inadequacy, dread, or self-doubt. It's a journey that calls for us to be willing to find out the darkish recesses of our brains, to do not forget the reasons within the back of our responses, and to undergo the ache that emerges at the same time as we deal with the motives of our self-unfavorable conduct.

A careful balancing act of introspection and self-compassion is important to find out hidden self-sabotage triggers. It is a warfare to appearance the patterns that seem inside the course of times of strain, trouble, or change and to grow to be detectives of our very own cognitive strategies. By spotting those triggers, we restore our employer, allowing us to take a second to suppose earlier than performing in area of reacting. This workout offers us the capability to exchange the manner we react, allowing us to swap risky behavior styles for more positive ones.

We start to resolve the internet of establishments linking these triggers to our emotional responses through the prism of self-consciousness. It's a workout that may be empowering however is likewise difficult because it requires openness and a readiness to face scars which have been saved concealed. But at the same time as we become privy to those covert triggers, we lessen their have an impact on on us. By redefining our dating with these triggers thru the approach of unmasking, we're better capable of manage the disturbing situations of lifestyles with a fresh enjoy of energy and mastery.

Chapter 3: Navigating Fear and Resistance

The adventure of self-discovery necessarily brings us to a fork in the street while fear and resistance act as implementing barricades. This intersection, which was stimulated via manner of using my very own existence critiques, illustrates a vital factor whilst the protection of familiarity and the uncertainty of progress collide. I decided that overcoming fear and resistance is not an clean undertaking; it calls for a severa experience that famous the complexities of the human thoughts and our deeply entrenched tendency to stay with what is familiar.

An ominous strain known as fear frequently poses as a protector of protection and tempts us to remain in familiar surroundings wherein threat is decrease. The dread of failure, the concern of being judged, and the worry of the unknown were all present as I traveled the course of self-discovery. These concerns held me imprisoned in a global that emerge as a long way from great, irrespective of the fact that they've been added approximately via shielding instincts.

I located that resistance, it simply is inspired by means of our propensity to avoid soreness and change, emerge as fear's truthful accomplice. It showed up as procrastination, justifications, and a propensity to shirk duty. I emerge as able to take away the difficult however crucial measures toward transformation due to the resistance's seductive justifications. However, this competition carried valuable insights, so it became more than most effective a strain to be defeated. It served as a guidepost, mentioning locations that required my hobby and in which, if I had the courage to overcome my personal inertia, I can also want to revel in increase and evolution.

It took me some time to triumph over my tension and resistance; there were fits and starts offevolved and spurts of self assure interspersed with retreats. It desired me to be inclined to push into pain and flow into towards the threshold of my comfort sector in opposition to the recommendation of my instincts. It required acknowledging how improvement frequently takes vicinity within the same locations wherein we enjoy uneasy.

Through this approach, I located an extremely good paradox: as soon as confronted, fear and resistance may also additionally act as catalysts for transformation. They have the functionality for boom inner of them and are truely watching for our popularity and care. I learned that those emotions had reminiscences as I confronted them head-on instead of searching for to avoid them. These memories blanketed stories of past mistakes, injuries, and regulations. By acknowledging those myths, I emerge as able to rewrite them and observe worry now not as a barrier however as a signal that I actually have emerge as approximately to develop.

I determined out thru navigating fear and resistance that increase is a dance among braveness and vulnerability in vicinity of a directly line. It includes accepting the anxiety and reluctance now not as enemies to be vanquished but rather as touring companions. On this avenue, setbacks are not screw ups however rather stepping stones, and accepting opposition is not a signal of weak spot however as an opportunity a danger to alter our technique.

This voyage has given me a deep appreciation for a way a protracted way humans may match to conquer imagined barriers. It has tested to me how every movement taken towards development, no matter how small, affords up to create a mosaic of empowerment. It's a way that calls for staying electricity—the belief that overcoming resistance and navigating worry consists of furthermore recognizing how they have got an effect on our alternatives.

Navigating fear and resistance stays a financial ruin in my adventure that adjustments as I do. This economic catastrophe has taught me to view those feelings now not as barriers to overcome but instead as compass factors that thing me within the route of my remaining capability. It serves as a tribute to the power of resiliency, the strength that comes from going through soreness head-on, and the beauty that arises whilst we dare to go into the unknown no matter resistance and worry.

Embracing Fear as a Catalyst for Growth

In the complicated web of my adventure, fear confirmed up as an unanticipated but powerful stimulant for development—a mentor shrouded in pain and uncertainty. I located out that accepting fear as a motivator for boom required a paradigm shift that examined my deeply held assumptions. Fear had constantly been a robust foe, putting the brakes on my dreams and aspirations and paralyzing me inside the face of the unknowable. But as I dug deeper into my very non-public story, I saw that worry has the capacity to push me above my constraints and inspire me to stretch, alternate, and redefine them.

The method of dealing with dread worried pauses, quivering braveness, and a strength of will to plunge into the unknown. It became now not a easy shift. I positioned myself at the verge of making alternatives that sparked a heady brew of dread and excitement. However, it changed into within the midst of this anxiety that I determined out a vital reality: fear became now not a few element to be triumph over but as an alternative a associate to be stated. It conveyed a message, a whisper, that resonated with the opportunity of development and trade.

As I started out out to absolutely obtain my fear, I understood that it emerge as the important aspect to exploring new regions of self-discovery. It served as a replicate, reflecting the bounds of my comfort vicinity and illuminating the bounds I had installation to protect myself from the unusual. The draw close of worry modified right into a reminder that I modified into approximately to enjoy boom in choice to an illustration of my frailty. It made me keep in mind essential troubles, in conjunction with: What lies past this worry? What opportunities lie on the opposite aspect of ache?

I had to alternate my attitude from avoidance to inquiry a great way to embrace fear as a stimulus for boom. It required me to engage in awkward conversations, pursue obligations that made my coronary heart race, and tackle barriers that appeared insurmountable. I observed out that, while recognized and controlled, worry would possibly probably act as a beacon, illuminating the way to my actual goals. It seemed as no matter the truth that I had located a mystery reserve of braveness that had commonly been there, truly ready to be launched.

I decided that growth have become no longer linear while faced with tension; as a substitute, it modified proper into a journey that superior in spirals of development and setback. It changed into about moving forward, no matter how slowly, and know-how that each step introduced me one step towards being a extra broader model of myself. As a reminder that development wasn't approximately perfection however alternatively about being willing to embody vulnerability and uncertainty, embracing worry demanded self-compassion.

Through this approach, I understood that embracing fear intended improving my connection with it in preference to really casting off it. Fear no longer served as a barrier, but alternatively as a passageway that took me from the referred to to the unknown. It served as a regular reminder that seeking out increase did not come without trouble, but that pain indicated that I turn out to be actively taking element within the method.

The numerous times in which fear and exuberance collide preserve to form my journey in the direction of accepting worry as a catalyst for improvement. This journey is a celebration of the human spirit's fortitude and a testomony to our excellent capability to convert issue into opportunity. It serves as a reminder that managing our fears head-on, accepting their presence, and allowing them to lead us towards our capacity are all crucial to growing. Through this beauty, fear stops being a roadblock and as an alternative transforms right into a beacon, illuminating the path to a existence lived with courage, honesty, and a constant quest for development.

Overcoming Resistance to Change

The system of overcoming resistance to exchange is complex and requires a cautious balancing act amongst introspection, flexibility, and resilience. Resistance frequently seems as a strong barrier, a defense in opposition to the uncertainties and discomforts that encompass exchange, within the tapestry of private progress. However, I've located from my personal experience that resistance is not an unbreakable strain but as an alternative a gateway to transformation that virtually need to be opened. In order to conquer our resistance to exchange, we want to delve deeply into the reasons of our problems and make a determination to rewriting the reminiscences that maintain us trapped in our comfort zones.

Self-focus, or an open evaluation of the fears and assumptions that manual our resistance, is step one in this approach. We can discover the underlying strategies that hold our resistance through difficult the intellectual patterns that adhere to the reputation quo. Resistance frequently consequences from a worry of failing, the unknown, or letting skip of control. As we tear down the restrictions that preserve us from trade, it takes compassion and a commitment to be kind to ourselves to triumph over the ones issues.

A deliberate attitude trade is crucial to triumph over resistance to alternate. It includes recasting trade as a possibility for boom, evolution, and increase. We begin to take down the partitions of resistance one brick at a time via specializing inside the potential blessings in vicinity of obsessing over the in all likelihood drawbacks. It's approximately accepting change as a manner of studying approximately oneself and embarking on a journey that takes us to new frontiers of increase and studying.

Additionally, it takes endurance and a willingness to consist of suffering to overcome resistance. Change is rarely easy; it often involves hiccups, diversions, and durations of uncertainty. It includes expertise that setbacks are not a sign of failure but as an opportunity vital steps within the manner. By training resilience, we assist our ability to face up to the storms of uncertainty and pop out stronger.

In my journey, getting over reluctance to alternate has been a constant exercising—a living example of the manner adaptable the human spirit is. It serves as a reminder that the street to alternate isn't always without troubles, however that each one gives room for improvement. We open the door to a life lived with purpose, honesty, and the endless opportunity that emerges from accepting trade via the use of dealing with resistance with braveness, hobby, and an unshakable strength of mind to development.

Chapter 4: Rewiring Limiting Beliefs

Untangling the deeply ingrained perception styles that have subconsciously created our thoughts-set of ourselves and our competencies is a essential step inside the reworking manner of rewiring proscribing beliefs. These ideals characteristic invisible obstacles that limit our development and functionality They are regularly derived from previous critiques, cultural training, or horrific self-communicate. In my personal personal development journey, I've discovered that transferring restricting ideals includes greater than simply converting our thinking; it additionally involves rewriting the recollections which have stored us captive and swapping them out for empowering ones.

The first step on this device is focus—an introspective research of the ideals that guide our alternatives and movements. We can find out the motives of those thoughts and the events that brought about them through way of dropping mild on them. This self-reputation lets in us to investigate the fact of those thoughts and decide whether or not or not they in reality replicate who we're as humans, which acts as a strong motivator for transformation.

A sensible strength of mind to self-compassion is essential for the adventure of rewiring proscribing ideals. It includes admitting that the ones views are the results of indoctrination in preference to reflections of our crucial values. We foster a supportive surroundings for trade via sporting out a kinder internal discourse. It's about breaking the loop of self-complaint that helps those restricting ideals and treating ourselves with the equal warm temperature and help that we freely offer to others.

Rewiring limiting thoughts moreover consists of growing a perspective on capacity. It includes actively searching out evidence that disproves the ones assumptions and developing a database of counterexamples. By reinterpreting our evaluations via the prism of opportunity and boom, we name into query the veracity of limiting beliefs and make room for fresh options.

This course moreover calls for persistent exercising and repetition. Rewiring restricting beliefs involves swapping out vintage affirmations for additonal powerful ones. It consists of building a highbrow environment that facilitates in preference to hinders our dreams. We create highbrow pathways to transformation through deliberately choosing to pay attention on exceptional self-speak and reinforcing self-setting forward thoughts.

Rewiring restricting thoughts has been freeing and hard for me in my opinion. These ideals have end up ingrained in our minds over time, so converting them requires persistence and resolution. But as I've not unusual this adventure, I've seen firsthand how effective transformation can be. The transformation happens no longer certainly in our thinking, however additionally in our deeds, picks, and possibilities.

Reclaiming oneself through the venture of rewiring one's restricting beliefs is evidence of the big energy our personal narratives hold over us. We input a worldwide of empowerment and functionality whilst we rewrite those narratives, unfastened from the load of our very own constraints. This voyage well-known the amazing plasticity of the human thoughts and its ability to go beyond preconceived notions and create a present day global. By accepting this machine, we deliver ourselves the possibility to live a life packed with sincerity, reason, and a employer believe in our non-public abilties.

Uncovering the Roots of Limiting Self-Beliefs

The layers of our beyond research, societal influences, and inner dialogues that have woven the complex tapestry of our self-belief must be deeply probed. that permits you to understand the origins of restricting self-ideals. My personal quest for self-discovery has led me to the belief that those ideas often carry out silently as the developers of our mind, emotions, and choices, performing below the floor. As this tool of unearthing forces us to face the memories, sports, and narratives that have original our experience of self, it necessitates a cautious balancing act of introspection and compassion.

In order to discover the motives of limiting self-ideals, we need to bravely find out our past. It entails exploring defining moments that have completely common our identity, every truly and negatively. We can turn out to be aware about the origins of beliefs which have both helped us increase or held us again via the usage of searching on the testimonies we've were given got internalized from our upbringing, interactions, and societal expectancies.

This voyage is likewise an possibility to test our internal conversations and venture the veracity of our self-perceptions of charge, aptitude, and functionality. These perspectives are regularly the surrender quit end result of judgments, comparisons, and beyond disasters. We can decide whether those stories are proper representations of our talents or simply stale scripts that we have were given everyday through time through confronting those narratives.

Finding the causes of restricting self-ideals consists of more than simply handling as a great deal as ugly research; it moreover involves recognizing any first-rate studies that could have been eclipsed thru the horrible ones. It consists of figuring out the accomplishments, affirmations, and resiliency that defy the limiting ideals. We can stability the scales and recast our self-belief to encompass a fuller, greater right depiction of who we're by using way of dropping moderate on these sports.

On my path, coming across the reasons of proscribing self-thoughts has been an act of self-compassion—a conscious try to understand that those beliefs are not the end result of innate defects but alternatively the results of complex occasions and conditions.

It's approximately allowing ourselves the liberty to replace the restricting memories we've got got been wearing round with ones that sell empowerment, improvement, and opportunities.

As proscribing thoughts may additionally additionally have deep roots, this quest requires patience. It requires a readiness to sit via ache and paintings through the emotions that ground as we're facing the reminiscences which have molded us. But thru going through this manner, we take once more manage of our self-narrative. Finding the resources of these mind lets in us to redefine who we're, query prolonged-held beliefs, and grow to be a extra real and increased version of ourselves. It's a adventure that has the strength to free us from the bonds of self-doubt and pave the way for a life characterized by means of manner of self-recognition, resiliency, and limitless possibility.

Challenging and Transforming Negative Thought Patterns

A profound adventure into the interior geography of our minds is needed to project and remodel harmful thinking patterns, and this journey has the capability to trade how we understand the arena, how we sense, and the way we behave. In my personal self-development research, I've determined that terrible idea patterns often act as covert developers of our reality, tingeing our stories with self-doubt, worry, and constraints. Self-focus, mindfulness, and self-compassion are all critical components of this transforming way as we paintings to loose up ourselves from the grip of recurring, counterproductive questioning.

The consciousness that our thoughts are not goal realities however as an possibility interpretations created with the resource of the usage of our studies and ideals sits on the center of this journey. Developing a vigilant focus of our inner conversations is step one in hard terrible concept patterns. We create a location for introspection—a pause to bear in mind the accuracy of our presumptions and if they're steady with our modern-day truth—through using objectively examining the ones mind.

To discover the reasons of those awful idea patterns, one need to actively pursue this tool. It includes tracing their origins—previous encounters, assessments, or comparisons that might have inspired their improvement. We acquire notion into the reminiscences which have saved us prisoner and have a look at the strands that may be untangled with the aid of the use of knowledge their origins.

Negative thinking styles want to be challenged and transformed, and they want to get replaced with tremendous, declaring ones. We deliberately select to reroute our questioning closer to greater impartial and uplifting viewpoints on this device of cognitive restructuring. We create new thoughts pathways that direct our minds in the direction of healthful interpretations through repetition and deliberate attempt.

In my personal adventure, I've found that self-compassion is an important best friend in this machine. If we need to trade our horrific concept styles, we need to be as kind to ourselves as we'd be to a pal. It consists of know-how that the ones patterns are the manufactured from observed behaviors that may be undone over time, in area of being a signal of private failure.

Furthermore, incorporating mindfulness into our each day lives is crucial for converting negative concept patterns. With the assist of mindfulness, we may additionally word our thoughts objectively and widely recognized their fleeting nature. By setting aside ourselves from our mind, we lessen their have an effect on over us, permitting us to react consciously in vicinity of reflexively.

This transformational journey is packed with each victories and disasters. It's a methodical machine that necessitates patience and staying electricity. But with the aid of the use of using making these attempts, we open the door for a massive exchange in how we see ourselves and the arena. We also can create a reality that is optimistic, self-confident, and characterized through a profound consciousness of the potential that lives internal us with the resource of confronting and reforming poor concept styles.

Chapter 5: Cultivating Self-Compassion

The most vital dating we have were given is the one we percent with ourselves, and cultivating self-compassion is a reworking journey that strengthens this relationship. Self-compassion is a effective strain that fosters resilience, self-popularity, and real thriving, as I've located out through my private journey of private improvement. This approach consists of giving ourselves the equal love, compassion, and statistics that we freely deliver to others. It's approximately embracing our humanity—acknowledging our flaws, disasters, and weaknesses—and responding with compassion and kindness.

The subject of self-reputation is the cornerstone of growing self-compassion. It entails becoming privy to our inner conversations, specifically the times when self-judgment and self-complaint infiltrate our mind. Through this information, we start to project the presumptions that underlie the ones intense judgments, thinking their validity. This focus additionally makes room for introspection, giving us a danger to renowned our annoying situations without judging ourselves as failures.

To increase self-compassion, we must alternate the way we interpret our tales. It entails changing one's mind-set from one in each of self-records and self-forgiveness to one of self-grievance. We open the door to a greater expertise and liberating courting with ourselves with the beneficial useful resource of information that mistakes are possibilities for improvement, setbacks are a important part of the adventure, and flaws are what make us human.

Additionally, adopting reputation is essential for this enjoy as it continues us within the gift and lets in us to check our mind objectively. Since it assists us in breaking the loop of vital and unkind self-communicate, mindfulness creates a conducive environment for the development of self-compassion. We can examine our emotions and memories with an open coronary coronary coronary heart while we exercise mindfulness.

My very very own experience shows that developing self-compassion is a brave act—a desire to area our intellectual fitness first and address ourselves with the identical kindness we do for others. It's a topic that alters how we cope with boundaries, failures, and self-doubt. By being type to ourselves, we create a resilient inner haven that protects us from existence's storms.

I've discovered thru this journey that working towards self-compassion is a lifelong employer in region of a very last vacation spot. It's a lifelong willpower to be there for ourselves in love, even if we're suffering or feeling inclined. It's a thorough act of self-want to make the strength of mind to deal with ourselves with the identical recognize as our cherished ones.

Self-compassion cultivation is an funding in our intellectual and emotional health. It's approximately figuring out that our intrinsic rate as humans determines our really worth, no longer our accomplishments, outward appearances, or assets of external validation. The door to a lifestyles lived with greater authenticity, self-popularity, and a profound enjoy of belonging—to ourselves, to others, and to the arena—is opened by means of way of the usage of cultivating self-compassion.

Practicing Kindness and Forgiveness Towards Yourself

I placed a remodeling exercising that would alternate the route of my adventure even as navigating the maze of personal development: displaying myself love and forgiveness. This epiphany wasn't the quit give up result of lofty aspirations however alternatively the unvarnished fact of my non-public studies. It emerge as a lesson found the tough way, after making numerous mistakes and having to stand my very non-public flaws. A lifeline that rescued me from the depths of self-complaint and guided me toward self-popularity become training kindness and forgiveness within the course of myself.

This journey began out with a sincere but large shift in factor of view. I stopped punishing myself for my mistakes and started out out to deal with myself with the identical kindness I might show a friend. Making the choice to replace self-criticism with self-know-how become planned. I commenced out to think to myself, "What could probable I say to a cherished one in this situation?" as I became navigating issues. This workout helped me close to the gap many of the empathy I withheld from myself and the compassion I freely provided to others.

It changed into critical to stand my flaws and regrets head-on on the way to exercise self-kindness and forgiveness. It have grow to be about spotting my humanness and the fact that I modified into nevertheless developing and vulnerable to make mistakes. It become a humbling and releasing adventure. It intended letting skip of the guilt I had carried round for far too lengthy and forgiving myself for beyond picks that had tormented me.

This exercising's incorporation of mindfulness changed right right into a vital development. I determined out the manner to don't forget of my mind and to observe them objectively, which allowed self-kindness to broaden. It concerned being aware of even as self-criticism crept in and actively determining to react with self-compassion in its vicinity. I located through mindfulness that education self-kindness supposed accepting my imperfections with a coronary coronary heart entire of compassion in vicinity of trying to disguise them.

Resilience come to be wished due to the truth the experience wasn't sincere; I needed to practice love and forgiveness in the path of myself. There have been times as soon as I would possibly start to criticize myself, propelled by means of evaluation or my fear of failing. But within the ones moments, I reminded myself that displaying kindness to oneself required willpower—a dedication to deal with oneself with the same apprehend and decency as one did in the course of others.

The voyage additionally modified how I treated failure and setbacks. I noticed them as stepping stones on the manner to boom, instead of permitting them to define me. When I made a mistake, I did not blame myself; as an alternative, I recognized the training I have to look at from the state of affairs. Through a trade in point of view, I became capable of rework hurdles into achievements thru seeing worrying situations as possibilities for studying.

In my very very own tale, forgiving and being type to myself acted as catalysts for internal recuperation. It changed into approximately converting the judgments that have been ingrained in my thoughts with affirmations of my fee as a person. It needed to do with showing myself the identical forgiveness that I ought to reveal someone else who had erred.

This experience wasn't clean; it needed self-consciousness and useful effort. However, the benefits were incalculable. I unlocked a wellspring of self-compassion which have turn out to be the cornerstone of my emotional well-being via schooling kindness and forgiveness toward myself. It have become an empowering journey that served as evidence of our wonderful capability to exchange the manner we see ourselves.

As I think lower again in this course, I see that forgiving and being type to your self is a manner of life, now not most effective a practice. It involves cultivating a loving, compassionate, and resilient relationship with oneself. In the midst of existence's upheaval, being patient with oneself—forgiving, recovery, and embracing the splendor of our unsuitable, developing selves—is one of the maximum powerful acts of courage. This path remains ongoing.

Breaking Free from Self-Criticism and Guilt

I set out in this voyage with the choice to liberate myself from the bonds of unrelenting self-complaint and guilt, but it required a large exchange in the topography of my internal lifestyles. This shift did no longer come about due to lofty mind however as an opportunity from the depths of my private troubles, in which the weight of beyond misdeeds and the strangling keep near of shame had faded my experience of self confidence. Confronting my internal critic—the ones echoes which have been continuously berating me for my perceived shortcomings and failures—changed into critical to liberate myself from self-complaint and guilt.

A vital first step in this road emerge as facts that my self-criticism and guilt had been now not supporting. I didn't suppress these emotions; alternatively, I allowed them to head back up, making room for open meditated photograph. It have become about searching into the recesses of my mind, discovering the motives of those emotions, and thinking about whether or now not they have been appropriate. Through this manner, I came to see that shame and self-complaint were unwelcome visitors that restricted my improvement and distorted my viewpoint.

I had to deliberately refocus my interest in order to get away self-complaint and guilt. I began out consciously that specialize in my traits, successes, and instances as soon as I had endured within the face of trouble. I labored on being compassionate with myself, treating myself with the identical apprehend I may additionally deliver a pal who changed into experiencing a comparable set of emotions. For this exercise, I had to deliberately rewire my intellectual strategies to transport them some distance from self-blame and in the direction of self-splendor.

On this ride, mindfulness changed into vital. I evolved present-moment popularity and discovered a manner to test my thoughts objectively. I found that dwelling at the past or speculating approximately the future regularly delivered about self-criticism and guilt. I modified into capable of ground myself in the right right here and now manner to mindfulness, which provided a destroy from the loop of complaint. It changed into a tool that enabled me to loose myself from self-judgement and adhere to readability.

Accepting the idea of forgiveness—forgiving myself—grow to be each extraordinary step in overcoming self-criticism and guilt. It concerned coming to phrases with the fact that I modified into nice human, at risk of errors, and deserving of mercy. This voyage required a planned preference to permit skip of the guilt that had grown to be a depended on tour companion. I became capable of get to the bottom of the tangles of my past and regain manipulate over my intellectual health with the resource of walking toward self-forgiveness.

In my private experience, the path to liberation worried letting flow of disgrace and self-grievance. It changed into about tearing down the mind that had imprisoned me, thoughts like "I am described thru using my mistakes, I am unworthy of kindness, and I am described thru my past actions." Although not with out its difficulties, this method required perseverance and self-attention. There were times after I felt the need to criticize myself once more, but with the assist of my newly determined equipment, I changed into able to get via the ones situations with resiliency.

This adventure of liberation from guilt and self-grievance served as a testomony to the transforming potential of self-compassion. I become capable of alternate the direction of my very very own story thru data that my price grow to be independent of the errors I had committed. Through this enjoy, I created a direction to self-empowerment that changed into characterised via self-popularity, fortitude, and a profound hobby that I changed into deserving of kindness, irrespective of my flaws. It's a manner that by no means ends, reminding me that letting skip of self-judgment and guilt requires greater than just guts; it additionally calls for reclaiming my personal story and identifying how I want to find out myself.

Chapter 6: Embracing Change and Uncertainty

Accepting exchange and uncertainty calls for a profound tango with lifestyles's erratic rhythms—a complex adventure that calls for adaptability, resiliency, and an open coronary heart. In my private quest for self-discovery, I've found that trade isn't always an remoted occurrence however as an alternative a regular partner. To definitely have interaction with alternate's current potential, one have to include it in location of actually tolerate it. Knowing that growth prospers in the fertile soil of uncertainty, it is a deliberate preference to allow pass of familiarity and flow into into the place of the unknown.

This adventure starts offevolved with a viewpoint adjustment—a change of trade from an uncomfortable source to a rich source of opportunity. Accepting exchange encourages us to look it as an engine for development, a doorway to uncharted regions with the capability for increase and evolution. It consists of understanding that soreness brought on with the aid of change frequently heralds the emergence of easy views, aptitudes, and opportunities.

Additionally, embracing trade necessitates developing resilience—the functionality to adjust and flourish within the face of ambiguity. A mindset that is open to gaining knowledge of and sees barriers as stepping stones rather than roadblocks fosters resilience. In order to include the pain as a signal that we're actively taking element inside the gadget of development, we need to muster the braveness to head away our comfort location and enter the area of trade.

An vital element of this route is gaining knowledge of to embody ambiguity. Like alternate, uncertainty is a herbal part of existence's tapestry. Accepting uncertainty involves letting skip of the call for for fact and locating comfort in the united statesand downs of life's rhythms as opposed to looking to exert manipulate over the uncontrollable. It's a shape of mindfulness—a planned choice to be discovered in each 2d, even if the way earlier is obscured with the resource of uncertainty.

My non-public revel in suggests that accepting trade and uncertainty has been each liberating and difficult. My route has taught me to allow go of my attachment to outcomes and instead admire the splendor of the triumphing. It includes growing a feel of self guarantee in my private ability to face the destiny with grace and resiliency in desire to based mostly on the predictability of my times.

There will certainly be uncomfortable, uncertain, and scary times along the way. But as I've ordinary alternate and uncertainty, I've additionally come to recognise that I already own a strength that most effective manifests while we face pain and trouble. It serves as a monument to the reworking power of accepting exchange and uncertainty because it famous the unexplored regions of our capacity, motivates us to upward push to the challenge, and cultivates a better courting with the dynamic internet of existence. Through this adventure, we come to apprehend that accepting alternate and uncertainty isn't actually a recall of surviving however additionally a announcement of our functionality to prosper, adapt, and preserve growing.

Harnessing Change for Self-Empowerment

The dynamic manner of harnessing trade for self-empowerment involves turning the winds of transformation right into a pressure that drives us towards extra improvement, authenticity, and resilience. In my very very very own adventure of private increase, I've discovered out that alternate can be used as an inner catalyst for empowerment in place of something that without a doubt occurs to us. This approach consists of accepting change as an opportunity to re-compare our pathways, push our limitations, and align with our actual potential in preference to as a disruption.

The expertise that exchange is a herbal a part of lifestyles and a clean canvas on which we also can moreover create our very very own tale is at the coronary heart of the use of trade for self-empowerment. It's about switching from a reactive to a proactive mind-set and figuring out to take manipulate of trade and direct it within the route of our goals. We assemble the idea for self-empowerment via way of accepting trade with an open mind and a growth-oriented thoughts-set.

It takes braveness to allow skip of the familiar and assignment into the unexpected in an effort to use trade for self-empowerment. It necessitates accepting soreness and uncertainty as paths to at the least one's very personal improvement. In doing so, we employ our natural potential to conform and get better from setbacks, permitting exchange to cultivate a sturdy enjoy of inner self belief and self-worth.

Self-empowerment thru change frequently involves recasting obstacles as possibilities. We selected to see disturbing situations as invitations for modern-day trouble-fixing rather than as insurmountable hurdles. This exchange in issue of view gives us the capacity to stand trade head-on, regular in the understanding that each obstacle is an opportunity to demonstrate our resourcefulness and staying power.

The notable potential of the human soul to decide its personal route has been verified in my private direction via manner of my functionality to apply trade for self-empowerment. It consists of developing a curious mind-set and exploring the opportunities that trade gives in vicinity of focusing on its alleged negatives. This adventure has not been with out problems; it has required self-recognition, flexibility, and a steadfast strength of will to development.

As I've used exchange to empower myself, I've located that the purpose of the manner isn't always to remove pain or issues; alternatively, it is to apply them as stepping stones to a extra empowered model of myself. Instead of stopping the beat of change, one should discover ways to dance with it. Through this dance, I've seen the development of my non-public fortitude and feature advanced a fresh statistics of the reworking capacity that lies inner instances of change.

This voyage is a announcement that, no matter the forces of alternate, we though have the strength to direct our lives. Adversity is converted into opportunity, uncertainty into possibilities, and pain into development at the same time as exchange is used for self-empowerment. It's a direction in the direction of taking manipulate of our very non-public future and accepting change as a co-conspirator in our quest for authenticity, which means, and a lifestyles lived consistent with our personal terms.

Thriving Amidst Uncertainty: The Path to Self-Mastery

The path to self-mastery is a reworking adventure outstanding via resilience, adaptability, and a profound records of our private capability. Thriving within the face of uncertainty is a journey marked with the resource of these features. I've found from my non-public journey of self-discovery that thriving in the midst of uncertainty is an artwork that requires a cautious balance amongst thoughts-set, self-interest, and planned motion. Embracing existence's ever-changing nature with an open coronary coronary coronary heart and a increase-orientated outlook is the vital detail to thriving in the face of uncertainty.

The know-how that uncertainty is a important trouble of life and an invite to sail uncharted waters with braveness in place of fear sits on the middle of this journey. Developing a mindset that sees obstacles as mastering opportunities, disasters as classes, and ambiguity as a smooth canvas for inventive edition is vital to thriving inside the face of uncertainty. It's approximately adopting a proactive in area of reactive mind-set and figuring out to apply uncertainty as a motivator for personal improvement.

Self-recognition, or the ability to tune into our mind, emotions, and behaviors, is essential for this path in the direction of self-mastery in the face of uncertainty. We can take a look at greater about our routine varieties of conduct, our triggers, and our default coping mechanisms through tracking how we react to uncertainty. This self-focus gives us the energy to make planned alternatives in desire to appearing involuntarily out of worry or tension.

Accepting soreness as a doorway to growth is a few other element of thriving in an uncertain worldwide. It consists of voluntarily venturing outside of our comfort region and taking on obligations that boom our abilties. We are capable of see our innate resilience and strength via this machine, which serves as a reminder that we're a protracted manner extra succesful than we normally supply ourselves credit score rating for. Our self-self perception grows as we step up to the plate and deal with adversity with grace, in addition advancing us in the direction of self-mastery.

In my very own journey, prospering in the face of ambiguity has been a testament to the extraordinary adaptability of the human spirit. It's about growing a revel in of employer over our responses and options, even in surprising conditions. This street has demanded humility because it requires us to surrender the illusion of manipulate and as an alternative placed our interest on developing our inner sources—our adaptability, inventiveness, and resilience.

Surviving in an uncertain worldwide isn't always an easy effort to address. It necessitates a readiness to face discomfort, a dedication to lifelong analyzing, and the notion that screw ups are sincerely stepping stones on the direction to achievement. Nevertheless, I've come to realize thru this direction that dominating ourselves in preference to outside situations is the genuine definition of self-mastery.

This adventure is a testomony to our potential to thrive no matter uncertainty in addition to our capability to stay to tell the tale its storms. We enter a location of self-mastery that is going past outside conditions as we learn how to encompass uncertainty as a trainer, a catalyst for improvement, and a easy canvas for transformation. This voyage exemplifies the meaning of personal empowerment by way of showing that regardless of modifications within the outside international, our indoors surroundings may also additionally though be a haven of electricity, resiliency, and infinite potential.

Chapter 7: Setting Purposeful Goals

Setting functional dreams is a deliberate adventure of goal and readability. In my private journey of personal improvement, I've determined that defining significant goals is greater than best a listing of desires; it is a avenue map that directs our movements, motivates us, and capabilities up our efforts with our ideals. This method consists of thorough studies of our hobbies, ideals, and aspirations in an effort to establish objectives which may be normal with our real selves.

The popularity that they skip beyond floor-degree desires and represent our number one values and the vision we have were given were given for our lives is on the concept of growing beneficial dreams. This adventure begins offevolved with reflected photograph—a look inner to discover what technique most to us, what energizes us, and what makes us feel fulfilled. We can also additionally lay the inspiration for goals that aren't exceptional externally pushed however moreover carefully tied to our enjoy of motive with the resource of the usage of knowledge our motivations and goals.

Setting intentional dreams consists of translating idealistic aspirations into feasible actions. It includes dividing our loftier desires into feasible, quantifiable objectives that direct our improvement. The steps, cut-off dates, and sources required to carry out every motive should be surely described, and this gadget calls for detail and readability. By cautiously planning our direction, we decorate our attention, strain, and responsibility.

Setting worthwhile goals additionally necessitates a boom-oriented thoughts-set, one that views obstacles as stepping stones at the route to mastery. It entails accepting that barriers and screw ups are critical elements of the experience and viewing them as possibilities for boom and development. This way of questioning no longer first-class gives us the energy to hold going at the equal time as matters get tough, however it additionally cultivates a spirit of resilience that drives us earlier.

In my personal revel in, setting up massive dreams has been a deliver of concept and steering. It includes developing a imaginative and prescient that transcends the regulations of the prevailing, directing our selections and moves with a enjoy of motive. This journey has known as for self-recognition as it calls for that we understand each our areas of strength and our regions for development, similarly to any capability roadblocks.

I've discovered out the transformational ability of sluggish development as I've set planned dreams. I revel in greater completed and benefit momentum with every step in advance, which allows me get toward my dreams. The potential we should actively create a future this is steady with our passions, values, and desires is hooked up via this voyage.

Purposeful motive-setting isn't with out its issues; it requires self-discipline, consistency, and the readiness to change course as important. I even have, however, felt the delight that comes from strolling in the route of goals which might be organically extensive, regular with my motive, and representative of the character I want to end up because of this way.

In give up, setting up meaningful dreams is a form of empowerment that affirms our inherent electricity to govern our very very very own futures. It's a journey that connects desires with successes, values with thoughts, and aspirations with reality. As we set out on this course, we enter a worldwide of cause-driven dwelling, in which our dreams aren't certainly a long way-off desires however actualized milestones that bypass us towards a existence of achievement, improvement, and enduring impact.

Defining Your Vision of Self-Mastery

A transforming voyage, defining your vision of self-mastery invites you to journey inside the direction of the massive expanse of your potential, values, and desires. In my personal journey of private development, I've discovered out that self-mastery is a dynamic manner of evolving into your top notch self in desire to a static holiday spot. This way includes delving deeply into your center values, regions of electricity, and areas for improvement, main to the appearance of a compelling imaginative and prescient that directs your choices and moves.

The recognition that self-mastery is a very non-public hobby sits at the center of setting up your imaginative and prescient of it. It's approximately coordinating your imaginative and prescient with who you in reality are—your passions, values, and particular competencies. This approach requires introspection—an open examination of your values, the subjects that clearly encourage you, and the form of legacy you wish to move away at the back of. You assemble the foundation for an honest vision through spotting your innermost aspirations and guiding thoughts.

Clarity—a enterprise grasp of who you need to be as someone and the form of lifestyles you want to live—is vital for outlining your imaginative and prescient of self-mastery. Your picks and actions may be guided thru this vision as a way to be consistent with your goals. Imagine the behaviors, connections, and successes that represent your adventure to mastery as you acquire a shiny image of the area you want.

Additionally, your self-mastery philosophy dreams self-control and tenacity. It's not just a passing concept; it is a enterprise strength of will to improvement and a strength of will to continuously decorate your capabilities, body of mind, and man or woman. This journey calls for a increase-orientated mind-set, one which sees obstacles as training opportunities and disappointments as stepping stones towards your goals. Adopting this mind-set will assist you acquire self-mastery via boosting your resilience and motivation.

In my personal enjoy, articulating my idea of self-mastery has been a call to discover the unrealized capacity I possess. It's approximately stepping out of doors of my consolation vicinity and developing abilties that skip beyond what I formerly believed modified into possible. Because it includes dealing with regions that need development and accepting the discomfort that includes change, this direction has required braveness.

As I've superior my definition of self-mastery, I've come to see that it isn't a goal to be attained however instead a lighthouse that directs my route. This vision motivates me to tackle issues, look for opportunities for development, and lead a values-primarily based absolutely life. It serves as a reminder that mastery is set regular boom, a self-discipline to being the wonderful model of myself, in place of perfection.

It calls for self-reflection, openness, and a willingness to alternate; defining your photograph of self-mastery isn't with out difficulties. However, with the useful resource of going through this technique, you're able to take manipulate of your tale and create a lifestyles this is entire of because of this, fulfillment, and significance. As you flow into in advance, your imaginative and prescient of self-mastery serves as a lighthouse to manual you and a reminder that the adventure to self-mastery is a remodeling one with the capability to decorate every your lifestyles and the lives of these spherical you.

What Is SMART?

Here is an outline of the SMART acronym:

Specific: There have to be no opportunity for ambiguity in the purpose; it ought to be smooth and precise. It provides a easy choice to the hassle of what exactly must be finished. For example, a specific cause is probably "I want to set up a constant each day workout ordinary," in preference to a wellknown one like "I want to decorate my lifestyles."

Measurable: A purpose that can be measured or tracked in some way is said to be measurable. Setting sure necessities to degree improvement includes this. This makes it possible to installation unique checkpoints and decide whilst the purpose has been reached. A measurable element, for instance, can be "I want to talk up hopefully in at least three group meetings within the subsequent month." If the purpose is to increase self-self belief.

Achievable: dreams are sensible and viable given the to be had time, sources, and different factors. It avoids putting in dreams which may be overly bold or not possible to attain. It establishes a hard but possible cause on the equal time as acknowledging one's present day situation. An potential goal is probably to complete a 5K event after a few months of guidance in region of try to run a marathon with none preceding training.

Relevant: The aim need to be constant along with your common desires and aspirations. It want to be huge and relevant in your quest for non-public development. It stops you from pursuing objectives which might be unconnected on your development as an entire or avert it. If the aim is to growth productiveness, a pertinent goal might be to complete a selected project that advances your prolonged-time period professional goals.

Time-bound: A cause that has a set ultimate date for very last contact is stated to be time-nice. This issue establishes a ultimate date for finishing the mission, growing urgency and heading off procrastination. A time-positive intention might be to observe novels within the next month, in place of intending to examine a particular amount of books in the end.

Creating SMART Goals to Overcome Self-Sabotage

A strategic and empowering approach for overcoming self-sabotage is setting SMART goals. This technique offers us the electricity to give up the conduct that obstruct our success. On my private non-public boom path, I've come to understand that overcoming self-sabotage wishes a deliberate and systematic plan, and SMART goals offer the framework to negotiate this difficult terrain. SMART dreams, which can be Specific, Measurable, Achievable, Relevant, and Time-sure, offer a street map for successfully reversing self-destructive behaviors.

The readability that comes from element is on the center of putting SMART goals to combat self-sabotage. It includes absolutely outlining your objectives and disposing of any threat for misconception. Understanding the self-destructive behaviors you need to save you and locating pleasant replacements for them are critical components of this technique. Defining the self-sabotage triggers and patterns paves the way for placing objectives that mainly deal with those problems.

Measurability is crucial at the same time as placing SMART desires to prevent self-sabotage since it lets in you to screen your improvement and apprehend your victories as you skip. Progress tracking no longer only will boom motivation but additionally sheds mild on how nicely your techniques are operating. Your goals have to be broken down into manageable chunks so that you can see how an extended manner you've got got come and make any important adjustments.

These desires must additionally be to be had. While pushing oneself is crucial, having unrealistic expectancies may moreover demoralize you. Self-sabotage need to be defeated thru incremental, lengthy-lasting reform. Setting sensible desires enables you advantage momentum as you triumph over smaller barriers, boosting yourself-efficacy and self warranty in the approach.

To save you self-sabotage, placing SMART goals calls for relevance—a robust alignment among your dreams and the wider photo of personal development. These dreams must be steady together along with your desire to overcome self-defeating behaviors and forge earlier within the route of a more powerful future. Making positive that your dreams are pertinent for your course will provide you with the electricity and sense of direction wanted to triumph over demanding situations.

Setting time limits for your dreams provides a critical responsibility aspect. Your path to overcoming self-sabotage will flow more without problems if you live endorsed and targeted with the aid of the use of setting closing dates on your SMART dreams. Time-certain goals make certain that you constantly take movement in the course of your selected surrender stop result with the useful resource of preventing procrastination and using you ahead with a revel in of urgency.

My personal revel in has demonstrated that using SMART desires to combat self-sabotage is a modern-day technique that enables me to take down the partitions I've built. This street demands pondered image, openness, and a dedication to change. I've come to be extra aware about the behaviors I want to exchange and the tactics I want to lease as I've set clean, quantifiable, sensible, relevant, and time-high-quality goals. This approach has given me the ability to prevent self-destructing, however it has additionally helped me sense in rate and on top of factors of my conduct.

It requires commitment, self-reputation, and a willingness to stand hard truths to create SMART desires to conquer self-sabotage. But via this method, I've come to apprehend that I in reality have the power to rewrite my very very very own tale and transfer out self-defeating behavior with deliberate ones that sell my development. These targets act as a compass, pointing me within the route of a future unfastened from self-sabotage—a future characterised thru empowerment, self-mastery, and the fulfillment of my full potential.

Chapter 8: Building Resilience and Persistence

A transforming path that develops resilience and staying strength gives us the skills to face the disturbing situations of life with grace, tenacity, and an uncompromising spirit. I've determined out from my personal journey of private growth that tenacity and resilience are talents that may be evolved thru planned attempt and a increase-oriented mentality. This adventure involves accepting setbacks as probabilities for getting to know, mastering model inside the face of adversity, and gaining the highbrow and emotional braveness to keep going in the face of demanding conditions.

Recognizing that setbacks are not boundaries to overcome but instead milestones on the way to self-discovery is at the center of growing resilience and tenacity. It includes converting our mind-set so that we now not regard limitations as insurmountable obstacles however as a substitute as precious schooling that beneficial useful resource in our development. In order to complete this system, one want to be prepared to experience pain, studies from mistakes, and bring together the resilience important to get higher even more potent than earlier than.

Having a boom-oriented attitude, or the conviction that our skills may be advanced with practice, is a vital factor of growing resilience and tenacity. It entails know-how that setbacks are possibilities for learning and improvement as opposed to signs and symptoms and signs and symptoms of failure. This way of thinking permits us to look problems as opportunities to develop, to push ourselves past our consolation zones, and to boom a feel of manage over our conditions.

Additionally, growing adaptability—the functionality to alternate our route of motion in response to changing conditions—is important for growing resilience and perseverance. It consists of preserving an open mind to glowing mind, being prepared to trade path even as essential, and accepting change as a important issue of the journey. By developing our functionality for flexibility, we beautify our capability to persevere even inside the face of uncertainty. This capability permits us pick out new paths ahead on the identical time as hurdles seem.

In my personal enjoy, growing persistence and resilience has been a transformational manner that has given me the electricity and clear up to face traumatic conditions. It's about finding strength in the face of boundaries and calling upon your internal resources to maintain getting into spite of setbacks. This enjoy has taught me that perseverance and resilience are about gaining knowledge of the way to cope with issues in location of seeking to avoid them.

As I've advanced my fortitude and staying power, I've come to recognize that disasters aren't signs and symptoms and signs and signs of incompetence however alternatively studying opportunities. Every time I confronted a mission, I found out to reframe it as an opportunity to strengthen my ability for resilience, refine my hassle-solving abilities, and increase the emotional fortitude to persevere. This exercising has made me recognize that growing resilience and perseverance includes greater than genuinely surviving storms; it moreover entails flourishing after them.

Building staying electricity and resilience is not without problems; it necessitates self-reflected picture, vulnerability, and a determination to private development. I even have, but, witnessed the metamorphosis that results from going thru challenges with courage and an unshakeable spirit on this adventure. It's an empowering journey that serves as a monument to the exquisite functionality of people to triumph over barriers, overcome trouble, and preserve going after their goals.

Developing Emotional Resilience inside the Face of Challenges

A large adventure that lets in us to traverse lifestyles's united states of americaand downs with grace, composure, and an extensive recognition of our feelings is the development of emotional resilience in the face of adversities. In my very own journey of self-discovery, I've come to recognize that emotional resilience isn't always about stifling or fending off uncomfortable emotions however alternatively about growing the inner fortitude to way them in a wonderful and healthy manner. This path includes growing the competencies to govern strain, get over failures, and keep equilibrium and health even in the face of adversity.

Recognizing that our emotions are actual and that they act as messengers to reveal records approximately our internal selves is vital to constructing emotional resilience. It includes learning to have a have a look at our emotions objectively, permitting them to come to the ground, and recognizing their presence. Self-recognition is essential for this method; it consists of developing a aware try and locate and contact our feelings, recognize their causes, and extensively diagnosed the outcomes they have got on our attitudes, movements, and contemporary health.

Healthy coping strategies that assist emotional fitness are part of developing emotional resilience. It's approximately learning techniques that help us cope with hard emotions in green strategies, which incorporates mindfulness, deep respiration, journaling, and getting assist from loved ones or experts. We acquire the skills crucial to control strain, anxiety, and crush without jeopardizing our emotional well-being via the ones sports.

Furthermore, the functionality to reframe troubles as possibilities for improvement and getting to know is crucial for constructing emotional resilience. It includes developing a increase-orientated mindset that sees troubles as temporary demanding situations in preference to irreparable failures. This manner of thinking allows us to appearance the first-class factors of tough conditions, to look at from our failures, and to use our feelings to our advantage in area of to motive us distress.

In my personal experience, constructing emotional durability has been a direction of empowerment and self-discovery. It's approximately forging a sturdy bond with my emotions, getting to know the art work of being attentive to what they've to mention, and navigating them with kindness and statistics. This experience has taught me that emotional resilience is ready having the sources and capability to address disturbing conditions in a balanced way, in place of being evidence in opposition to them.

The functionality to preserve vicinity for difficult emotions and react to them in a way that promotes well being is what I've positioned to be important for developing emotional resilience. Vulnerability, self-compassion, and a strength of will to increase had been critical on this path. It's approximately developing the capacity to enjoy the emotional waves, figuring out that they pass speedy and that we've got got manipulate over how we react to them.

It can be hard to assemble emotional resilience; it calls for patience, introspection, and the capacity to tolerate suffering. However, inside the route of this path, I've come to understand the transformative capability of looking after my mental fitness. It's an empowering journey that demonstrates our functionality to boom emotional resilience, manage our responses to issues, and nurture a revel in of equilibrium, energy, and well being however the uncertainties of existence.

Persevering Through Setbacks: The Resilient Mindset

By overcoming boundaries with a resilient attitude, we may additionally display the high-quality strength we each personal and bypass forward in the face of trouble. In my very private journey of private development, I've located that setbacks are not limitations to growth but as an alternative opportunities for it, and that developing a resilient mind-set permits us to apply the ones problems as stepping stones in the direction of our desires. This adventure requires cultivating the intellectual and emotional durability to stand barriers head-on with braveness and remedy. It also calls for perceiving setbacks as quick detours rather than irreversible screw ups.

Recognizing that setbacks are a important hassle of any street in the direction of achievement is the cornerstone of overcoming barriers with a resilient mentality. It's about reinterpreting screw ups as pauses that supply us time to gather ourselves, reevaluate, and modify our approach. This approach requires a growth-orientated mind-set, or the conviction that setbacks aren't disasters however rather profitable getting to know opportunities that improve our non-public boom.

The capability to recover from setbacks and troubles is a essential issue of persevering through difficulties with a resilient mentality. It includes recognizing our feelings, digesting them, and then the usage of them as gas for our electricity of will. Instead of looking to govern our emotions, learning to channel them into super sports and responses is the key to developing this resilience.

Furthermore, adaptability—the functionality to trade our techniques at the same time as confronted with sudden obstacles—is critical for persevering thru screw ups with a resilient thoughts-set. It involves identifying that setbacks often necessitate a change in mind-set, a rethink of our techniques, and a readiness to go through in thoughts clean techniques. By being adaptable, we enhance our capability to exchange path and take one in every of a kind paths to our goals.

In my very private revel in, maintaining a resilient mind-set at the same time as overcoming setbacks has been a transformative adventure that has allowed me to conquer obstacles with grace and tenacity. Finding the high quality in setbacks, records the classes they'll train us, and the use of them to spur boom are key. I've determined from this route that setbacks are brief durations that permit us to growth stronger and wiser.

I've come to understand that I genuinely have effect over how I reply to problems because of persevering through setbacks with a resilient thoughts-set. This avenue needs self-compassion, self belief in my very very own abilities, and the remedy to maintain transferring ahead even if the going receives tough. It involves fostering the conviction that boundaries aren't the quit of the road but instead a necessary step inside the manner.

It calls for braveness, staying power, and a agency belief that we can conquer limitations and persevere via screw ups with a resilient attitude. But for the duration of this journey, I've witnessed the transformation that effects

from going thru demanding situations head-
on and with courage. It's a tale of resiliency,
demonstrating how resilient people can be in
the face of adversity, studies from failure, and
hold shifting earlier with unflinching strength
and remedy.

Chapter 9: Tools for Transformation

"Tools for Transformation" consists of some of beneficial and insightful materials those resource humans on their trips of self-discovery and personal improvement. These sources act as partners, catalysts, and guides to help humans exchange their attitudes, behavior, and lives. They include a big type of strategies, strategies, and ideas which are designed to promote increase and collect a better bond with one's real self. The use of affirmations, visualization physical video games, cause-setting frameworks, self-care strategies, journaling, emotional intelligence development, and hassle-solving techniques are a few examples of these gear. Every tool helps humans as they negotiate the terrain of self-development, create resilience, and recognize their whole potential, adding to the difficult tapestry of transformation.

Mindfulness and Meditation for Self-Mastery

The powerful strategies described in "Mindfulness and Meditation for Self-

Mastery" permit humans to growth internal attention, emotional manage, and a strong bond with their actual selves. Observing thoughts and feelings without passing judgment is a key trouble of mindfulness. On the opportunity hand, meditation offers an prepared technique for education consciousness and regularly incorporates strategies like centered attention or loving-kindness meditation. These strategies have the energy to transform people because they sell a greater experience of self-recognition, which makes it viable for humans to apprehend and damage loose from self-destructive belief styles.

Through mindfulness and meditation, people can discover ways to reply to difficulties lightly and rationally in area of . These strategies assist one understand the subtleties in their thoughts, emotions, and reactions, in the end giving them the freedom to choose thoughtful responses. As a end result, human beings are higher capable of address their fears, doubts, and uncertainties while growing sturdy, impartial questioning.

The practices of meditation and mindfulness help lay a strong foundation for self-mastery. They make it a great deal much less difficult to discover one's inner international, revealing proscribing thoughts and giving one room to change them. People can escape the hold of self-sabotage, accept change with composure, and direct their lives in the route of real boom and fulfillment through manner of cultivating a sturdy connection with the existing second.

Journaling: Unleashing Your Thoughts for Positive Change

Developing a talk with oneself through this exercise makes it less complex to research thoughts and feelings, respect successes, and technique losses with objectivity. Journaling fosters a experience of self-focus that evokes powerful exchange through recording accomplishments and education discovered out. Reflection permits people to recognize recurrent challenge subjects, recognise triggers, and unearth hidden reasons, in the end facilitating the alternate of unproductive idea behavior into efficient ones.

Chapter 10: Sustaining Self-Mastery for Life

I set out at the tough journey of Maintaining Self-Mastery for Life with each solve and humility. Self-mastery is a lifelong dedication to development, self-awareness, and intentional dwelling, as I've found out from my course. I've determined out through the highs and lows of my evaluations that keeping self-mastery calls for a robust determination to the mind and workouts which have helped me on my adventure towards non-public development.

Self-mastery first appeared like a lofty purpose—a choice to stand as much as self-sabotage, modify restricting beliefs, and amplify resilience. I placed that self-popularity is the first step—being willing to stand my fears, take shipping of my weaknesses, and cherish my strengths. It's about expertise that the street to self-mastery is a in no way-completing approach of improvement, a self-discovery dance that takes region through the years.

I came to apprehend the significance of consistency as I observed greater about keeping self-mastery. Making new behaviors a ordinary a part of my each day normal is extra essential than actually adopting them. My anchors, mindfulness and meditation, helped me live within the gift and negotiate the troubles of lifestyles with extra readability. Journaling superior proper into a confidante for me, a area wherein I may additionally need to type via my mind, renowned my accomplishments, and set desires.

In order to maintain self-mastery, one should be dedicated to lifelong mastering. I searched for publications, seminars, and mentors who should make bigger my attitude and provide sparkling perceptions. Being willing to constantly be a pupil turned into humbling, but it enabled me to enlarge and encompass new thoughts into my adventure. Through this manner, I got here to understand that improvement is not linear however alternatively involves a number of detours and turns that weave together to shape a self-mastery tapestry.

The potential to be compassionate with oneself became possibly the most influential lesson in retaining self-mastery. I discovered to deal with myself with care and tolerance due to the truth I realized that failures are a critical part of the course. This mind-set change become a turning element as it gave me the functionality to conquer barriers with extra resiliency, to look errors as analyzing opportunities, and to increase a business enterprise feel of my non-public rate.

Self-mastery is not with out problems. There were instances after I doubted how some distance I had come or ran into antique, self-defeating conduct. However, the ones instances served as a nicely timed reminder that self-mastery requires exercise rather than perfection. The motive of the revel in is to discover ways to cope with flaws with grace and compassion in area of in reality disposing of them.

I feel a high-quality revel in of appreciation as soon as I assume lower back on my avenue within the course of keeping self-mastery for the rest of my life. I now feel deeply linked to my internal self, unwaveringly assured in my competencies, and entire of newfound strength manner to this adventure. It has proven me that achieving self-mastery requires consistent electricity of mind to enhancing oneself. It is not a vacation spot that may be reached and checked off.

A tribute to the tenacity of the human soul is the capability to maintain self-mastery for existence. It involves accepting the difficulties, rejoicing inside the accomplishments, and figuring out that development is an ongoing technique. This course has taught me that self-mastery is an ongoing approach that is fabricated from pretty a few reviews and activities. It serves as a reminder that irrespective of the trouble of the journey, the very last tour spot is constantly inside attain and honestly organized to be decided for the primary time with every new step.

Integrating Self-Mastery into Your Daily Life

I undertook the transforming task of integrating self-mastery into your each day lifestyles with a mix of delight and apprehension. I decided from this revel in that achieving self-mastery entails making conscious selections, developing wholesome behavior, and adopting mindsets which have an impact on every component of our lives. Through the highs and lows of my very very very own reviews, I've come to apprehend that self-mastery is not a solitary challenge; as an alternative, it consists of incorporating increase, recognition, and intentionality into the very fabric of our normal exercises.

Aiming to overcome self-sabotage, enhance my wondering, and cultivate perseverance within the face of troubles, integrating self-mastery into my every day life first of all regarded like a frightening mission. But as I dug deeper, I got here to appearance that this journey begins with the ordinary, small movements anyone take each day. It's about setting up the mood for the day with the resource of beginning every morning with a few moments of mindfulness. It's about fostering empathy, bringing purpose to our encounters, and drawing near even the maximum routine chores with presence.

I determined that self-care modified into a important cornerstone as I carried on incorporating self-mastery into my each day lifestyles. Making sleep a priority, feeding my body wholesome meals, and exercise frequently built a basis of vigor that facilitated my development. I observed that when I took holistic care of myself, I come to be better capable of control problems and failures with grace and fortitude.

Making deliberate options inside the face of distractions changed into each different requirement for integrating self-mastery into my every day existence. Technology, demanding schedules, and outdoor pressures can resultseasily draw our cognizance faraway from the exercises that promote boom. Making time for self-mirrored image, journaling, or meditation is important because of the reality those sports assist us live anchored within the middle of pressure and stay in touch with our internal selves.

This voyage additionally forced me to reexamine my boundaries and relationships. It have emerge as vital for me to be round folks that encouraged and supported my growth. I developed the functionality to explicit my necessities, set up sound limitations, and allow flow into of connections that impeded my development. By cultivating healthful relationships, I created a placing that supported my quest for self-mastery.

Setbacks and issues had been unavoidable when I tried to consist of self-mastery into my every day existence. There were times when self-doubt started out out to set in, vintage sports activities reappeared, and the pull of comfort zones beckoned. But those times modified into possibilities to work on resilience and self-compassion. They helped me bear in mind that setbacks were not a sign of failure but alternatively part of the human revel in, a risk to choose myself up and preserve going.

The awareness that self-mastery is ready accepting imperfection with grace as opposed to accomplishing a static usa of perfection may additionally were the most profound. It entails accepting that development is an ongoing technique that involves a dance amongst successes and screw ups. I changed into capable of greet each day with a sparkling feeling of humility and hobby way to this attitude, appreciating the lessons that every event had to educate me.

The interconnection of the whole thing moves me as I assume decrease decrease lower back on my journey of incorporating self-mastery into my every day lifestyles. It consists of constructing a thoughts-set of growth and purpose that permeates each movement, choice, and come across, in place of actually carrying out meditation or writing sports activities. It serves as a reminder that self-mastery is a lifelong area that penetrates our lifestyles and imbues it with which means that, authenticity, and success.

Self-mastery Integration into each day lifestyles is proof of the effectiveness of persistent attempt. Realizing that private development is a adventure that takes location inside the cloth of our every day lives, rather than an remoted company, is the purpose. This revel in has taught me that even the tiniest moves should have a remarkable ripple impact if they may be finished with mindfulness and purpose. It's an invite to live according with the mastery that lies interior each mother and father, to appearance the mundane as an opportunity for progress, and to provide each day reason.

Creating a Supportive Environment for Continued Growth

Creating a Supportive Environment for Continued Growth has finished a massive position in my personal path, which has been each hard and fruitful. I positioned out from this chapter that prolonged-time period development requires a supportive and empowering environment so that you can flourish. As I started out in this journey, I got here to apprehend that our capacity for increase and self-mastery is fashioned with the aid of the use of the humans we spend time with, the environments we live in, and the impacts we deliver get entry to to.

Creating a supportive place of job first of all appeared like a big assignment. It entailed reviewing my relationships to decide whether or not they supported or impeded my dreams. It necessitated tough discussions and alternatives, on the aspect of on occasion letting skip of connections that have been now not supportive of my development. I decided out the importance of connections that are actual via this approach. It have end up important for me to surround myself with those who supported my journey—pals, mentors, and loved ones who had fun in my accomplishments and supported me within the path of disappointments.

Creating a conducive environment for ongoing boom protected my instant surroundings. I came to apprehend that our environment could in all likelihood mirror our inner states and function an impact on our movements and mind. I became able to create an area that fostered recognition, creativity, and contemplation by using the use of method of getting rid of clutter, arranging my surroundings intentionally, and which includes positivity. My dedication to development became reinforced through the usage of the ones minor changes, which helped it emerge as an important thing of my normal existence.

This chapter additionally clarified the importance of boundaries. I found the manner to shield my priorities, time, and energy from outdoor pressures that might reason me to veer off direction. It required pronouncing "no" to responsibilities that conflicted with my beliefs and "positive" to tasks that promoted growth. I included my time for self-care, training, and introspection thru establishing barriers—pillars that supported my direction to self-mastery.

Realizing that the net global is likewise part of our surroundings have end up in all likelihood the most poignant popularity. Our thoughts and feelings are formed thru social media, information, and digital content material cloth. I became aware of the importance of making an encouraging and powerful on line region through following payments that benefited my growth technique and unfollowing individuals who promoted negativity or assessment.

I confronted troubles and instances of uncertainty as I made my way inside the course of the landscape of establishing a welcoming surroundings for ongoing boom. There had been instances on the equal time as strain from the outdoor collided with my internal compass, inflicting turmoil internal. However, those sports allowed me to affirm my determination to development and self-mastery. They made me extra determined to position my very personal needs and development in advance of these of others or flimsy desires.

Making options which can be consistent with our real selves and desires is the crucial thing to fostering an environment that fosters continuing progress. It is a everyday system of evaluation, change, and reaffirmation in place of a unmarried movement. This financial ruin taught me that adjusting the out of doors factors which have an impact on us and ensuring that they aid our journey is also an essential part of boom.

I'm stimulated through the big have an effect on it has had on my path once I expect once more on my experience of constructing a supportive environment for ongoing boom. The people, locations, and impacts I've commonplace into my lifestyles have grown into pillars of energy which have helped me conquer barriers and feature an awesome time my victories. I placed out from this bankruptcy that positivism, genuineness, and cause create an environment in which boom can flourish.

The strength of deliberate options is tested through the ability to foster an surroundings that promotes ongoing improvement. Realizing that we've were given manage over the elements that have an effect on our lives and that by means of manner of developing an surroundings that encourages increase, we also can maximize our capacity for self-mastery, This enjoy has taught me that, at the same time as out of doors variables do play a element, it's far our internal strength of will and aware picks that circulate us in the route of continual improvement, authenticity, and a life of meaning.

Stepping proper right into a Transformed and Empowered Self

"Stepping right into a Transformed and Empowered Self" marks the give up of a considerable adventure that became characterized via self-focus, development, and a continuing quest for self-mastery. This turning point captures the inner metamorphosis similarly to the newfound revel in of empowerment that spills outward. It represents the culmination of severa instances of introspection, tenacity, and planned movement.

Stepping proper into a converted and empowered self is a testimonial to the willpower to growth—a determination that necessitated going thru fears, destroying self-terrible behavior, and rewriting restricting ideals. Embracing exchange as a stimulus for personal improvement and seeing setbacks as stepping stones inside the direction of success had been key components of this adventure. I've come out of all of it with a more experience of self-recognition, a clearer draw near of my values, and a sturdy connection to my real self.

A effective enjoy of empowerment—one which effects from expertise I definitely have the strength to govern my destiny—marks this critical 2d. It's approximately the use of the strategies, sports activities, and values I've developed to face barriers in lifestyles with grace and resiliency. Beyond private development, this empowerment gives you the capability to uplift others, make a tremendous impact on the arena, and depart an extended-lasting legacy of trade.

The adventure does no longer end when you step into your converted and empowered self; as an alternative, it marks the begin of a present day chapter that is characterized with the useful resource of intention, authenticity, and a revel in of course. It consists of making use of the understanding acquired, the statistics reached, and the self-mastery attained to every aspect of lifestyles. This encounter serves as a reminder that boom is a non-stop approach that develops as we welcome new stories, reason higher, and assignment into unexplored territory.

I'm thankful for the adventure that led me here as I take a step into my transformed and empowered self. The street referred to as for dedication, self-compassion, and the readiness to face discomfort. This 2d celebrates the resiliency of the human spirit and suggests that we're able to overcoming barriers, rewriting our memories, and taking courageous steps proper proper right into a destiny that is characterised through honesty, empowerment, and self-mastery.

Chapter 11: The Power of Self-Reflection

In pursuing non-public increase and self-improvement, a frequently-underestimated but pretty robust tool is to be had to us all: self-pondered image. It's the act of turning the lens inward, of reading our mind, movements, and evaluations deliberately and contemplatively. While self-reflected picture can encompass a sizable form of practices, one especially impactful method is growing a private success mag. Within the pages of this mag, you now not only report your adventure but furthermore discover valuable insights into your psyche, behaviors, and, positive, even yourself-sabotaging inclinations.

Creating a Personal Success Journal: Your Path to Self-Understanding

A non-public achievement mag is greater than best a diary of your each day sports sports; it is a dynamic tool designed that will help you develop and evolve. The machine starts offevolved with deciding on a journal that resonates with you and invitations you to region your mind on paper without a doubt. This mag serves as a sacred vicinity in which you may chronicle your desires, achievements, setbacks, and, most significantly, your journey of self-discovery.

1.   Setting Clear Intentions: Begin your magazine by way of setting clean intentions. What do you need to gain thru this workout? Is it to conquer self-sabotage, beautify your vanity, or chart your development in the direction of a particular cause? Having a smooth reason in your magazine publications your reflections and offers your efforts consciousness.

2.   Daily Reflections: Dedicate a part of every day to journaling. Consistency is essential, whether in the morning to set intentions for the day or within the night to reflect on what transpired. Document your mind, feelings, and critiques without judgment.

three. Goal Tracking: A private success magazine is an excellent region to tune your dreams. Write down your short-time period and lengthy-term aspirations, and often replace your improvement. This keeps you responsible and offers a tangible file of your achievements.

Analyzing Past Self-Sabotage Instances for Growth

Now, allow's delve into the coronary coronary coronary heart of self-reflected photograph - studying beyond self-sabotage instances for increase. Self-sabotage can take many office work, from procrastination and self-doubt to negative self-speak and worry of achievement. To efficiently fight those behaviors, it's miles important to confront them head-on and take a look at from them.

1.   Identify Self-Sabotaging Patterns: As you evaluation your magazine entries, pay unique attention to moments while you may have sabotaged your development. Look for ordinary topics, triggers, and conditions that reason self-sabotage. Were there unique

thoughts or emotions that surfaced all through the ones times?

2. Explore the 'Why': Once you've diagnosed self-sabotaging styles, dig deeper to apprehend the underlying 'why.' What fears, insecurities, or limiting beliefs may be riding those behaviors? By pinpointing the idea reasons, you could begin to deal with them efficaciously.

three. Seek Alternatives: With insights out of your magazine, brainstorm possibility behaviors and techniques to counter self-sabotage. For instance, when you have an inclination to procrastinate even as confronted with a daunting challenge, discover strategies which include time control, breaking duties into smaller steps, or seeking out of doors duty.

4. Track Progress: As you put into effect those options, use your magazine to tune your development. Note any changes in your mind, emotions, and behaviors as you parent to overcome self-sabotage. Celebrate small

victories along the way, and do no longer be discouraged with the aid of the use of occasional setbacks.

In end, the strength of self-reflected photo, through developing a non-public fulfillment magazine and analyzing past self-sabotage instances for increase, is a transformative adventure of self-discovery and development. It's a tool that lets in you to polish a mild at the shadows indoors, understand your self more deeply, and in the long run, ruin unfastened from self-sabotaging behaviors. Remember that this manner takes time and staying power, but with dedication and perseverance, you will discover yourself on a direction to greater self-interest and lasting pleasant trade. So, pick up that magazine and start writing to a higher, greater empowered you.

Setting and Celebrating Milestones: Making Progress Tangible

In the grand tapestry of private improvement and self-improvement, few matters are as vital as placing and celebrating milestones. These stepping stones pave the manner for lasting trade, helping you navigate the frequently winding street of transformation. In this bankruptcy, we are going to delve deep into the paintings of installing vicinity possible checkpoints and the importance of worthwhile yourself while you hit the ones milestones. By the give up, you will apprehend why milestones depend and a way to influence them to be simply proper for you.

The Significance of Milestones

Before diving into the practical components of putting and celebrating milestones, allow's first find out why they're so vital in pursuing self-sabotage prevention and personal boom.

1. Clarity and Direction: Milestones offer a roadmap for your journey. They wreck down your very last motive into smaller, functionality components, making the route forward a first-rate deal much less daunting.

2. Motivation and Momentum: Achieving milestones offers a enjoy of achievement and a motivational improve. These small victories can remind you of your progress, propelling you in advance while limitations appear.

three. Accountability: When you area milestones, you create a feel of duty. You have tangible targets to satisfy, making assessing your strength of mind and determination to your desires less complicated.

4. Measurement of Progress: Milestones act as benchmarks toward which you can diploma your improvement. They assist you track how far you have got come and how close to you're to reaching your ultimate reason.

Let's discover a manner to correctly set and characteristic a exquisite time those essential waypoints in yourself-sabotage prevention adventure.

Establishing Achievable Checkpoints

1.   Be Specific

Milestones ought to be precise and well-described. Instead of setting a indistinct goal like "save you self-sabotaging," smash it down into measurable additives. For example, you would likely vicinity a milestone like "perceive and replace one self-sabotaging conduct in the subsequent month."

1. Make Them Realistic

While ambition is admirable, setting unrealistic milestones can motive frustration and demotivation. Ensure your milestones are ability within the given time frame and resources. Gradual improvement is frequently greater sustainable than looking to carry out an excessive amount of too speedy.

1. Set a Timeline

Establish a smooth time body for carrying out each milestone. Having a final date creates a feel of urgency and stops procrastination. It furthermore allows you test whether or not or no longer you are making good enough improvement.

1.   Prioritize and Sequence

Consider the logical series of milestones. Some may also want to be finished earlier than others grow to be feasible. Prioritize them consequently to ensure a clean improvement toward your remaining goal.

Rewarding Yourself for Hitting Milestones

Setting milestones is nice 1/2 of the equation; celebrating them is further critical. Rewards not simplest extensively recognized your achievements but moreover enhance tremendous conduct. Here's the way to pass approximately it:

1.   Choose Meaningful Rewards

Your rewards need to align together together with your private opportunities and values. A tip that is significant to you may characteristic a effective motivator. It can be as easy as treating yourself to a favorite meal or taking a time off to relax.

1.   Celebrate Sincerely

When you attain a milestone, take some time to celebrate your accomplishment absolutely. Acknowledge the attempt and willpower it took to get there. Share your success with friends or circle of relatives who useful resource your journey.

1.   Reflect and Adjust

After celebrating, take a second to mirror for your development and the path beforehand. Use this reflection as an opportunity to modify your goals and milestones as desired. Your adventure is dynamic, and adapting alongside the way is okay.

1.   Avoid Self-Criticism

Lastly, avoid the lure of self-criticism if you encounter setbacks or miss a milestone. Self-improvement is a technique, and coffee stumbles are part of the journey. Instead of dwelling on screw ups, interest on studying and readjusting your technique.

In end, placing and celebrating milestones is a dynamic and empowering system that may appreciably beautify your self-sabotage prevention efforts. By setting up ability checkpoints and worthwhile yourself for hitting them, you're making improvement tangible and infuse your journey with motivation and positivity. Remember, every milestone reached is a testimony for your increase and resilience on the route to self-improvement. So, set those milestones and feature a extremely good time your adventure closer to a higher, more fulfilled you.

Accountability Partnerships: How Sharing Progress Boosts Success

Have you ever have been given all the way down to gather a significant motive, simplest to lose motivation and slip lower back into antique behavior along the way? If so, you aren't on my own. The journey towards private boom and self-improvement can be tough, and it is straightforward to get derailed by way of the use of self-doubt or procrastination. This is wherein the idea of obligation partnerships comes into play. By sharing your improvement and maintaining every first rate responsible, you can drastically enhance your possibilities of Success. In this text, we are able to delve into the advantages of duty pals and offer techniques for effective take a look at-ins to ensure that your responsibility partnership becomes a powerful tool in your self-sabotage prevention toolkit.

Chapter 12: The Benefits of Accountability Buddies

Before we dive into the techniques for powerful test-ins, allows discover why responsibility partnerships are so powerful in boosting Success:

1. Motivation Amplification: When you have got was given a responsibility partner, you are answerable to yourself and someone else. This added layer of duty can provide a powerful motivator to stick to your dreams and stay heading within the proper course.

2. Increased Commitment: Knowing someone is relying on you could substantially boom your dedication on your goals. You're an awful lot a lot less in all likelihood to hotel to procrastination or self-sabotage at the same time as a person is predicated on your development.

3. Real-Time Feedback: Accountability partners can offer treasured insights and feedback on your adventure. They can provide a glowing attitude, propose

alternative techniques, and help you navigate boundaries you may not have seen.

four. Celebrating Success Together: Achieving desires is greater amusing even as you may have amusing with someone who is familiar with the strive you have got mounted. Sharing your successes together in conjunction with your obligation companion can encourage and satisfy you.

5. Emotional Support: The adventure of self-improvement can be emotionally taxing at times. Having someone to percent your highs and lows with can offer emotional useful resource and help you live resilient within the face of challenges.

Strategies for Effective Check-Ins

Now that we've got explored the benefits of duty partnerships allow's communicate a way to make your take a look at-ins alongside side your duty companion as effective as viable:

1. Set Clear Expectations: Define your dreams and expectancies for the partnership

from the outset. What are you each hoping to reap? How frequently will you test in? What techniques of conversation will you operate? Clarity is critical to a a fulfillment partnership.

2.   Regular Communication: Consistency is vital. Set a schedule to your check-ins, whether or no longer it's far every day, weekly, or monthly. Stick to this time desk as intently as feasible to maintain momentum.

three. Share progress Honestly: Be open and honest approximately your development, even in case you've confronted setbacks. Transparency is critical for obligation to paintings correctly. If you're suffering, your associate can provide help and guidance.

four. Set SMART Goals: Ensure that your desires are Specific, Measurable, Achievable, Relevant, and Time-certain (SMART). This makes it a good deal less complicated to tune improvement and presents clarity on what Success looks like.

five. Problem-Solve Together: Use your accountability accomplice as a sounding board while encountering limitations or demanding situations. Brainstorm answers collectively and adapt your approach as wanted.

6. Celebrate Achievements: Don't neglect to rejoice your successes, no matter how small they'll appear. Acknowledging your development can enhance motivation and keep a powerful outlook.

7. Offer Constructive Feedback: Be supportive and tremendous on your feedback. Avoid judgment or criticism, and recognition on how you may help each distinctive decorate.

8. Adjust as Needed: Life is dynamic, and your dreams may also moreover trade. Be open to adjusting your goals and techniques as your adventure progresses.

In give up, obligation partnerships are a effective device for stopping self-sabotage and carrying out personal desires. By harnessing the advantages of having an responsibility pal and enforcing powerful take a look at-in techniques, you can drastically growth your opportunities of Success to your adventure of self-development. So, do not hesitate to are seeking out a like-minded accomplice and embark on this transformative journey together. Remember, your Success is best a partnership away!

Data-Driven Self-Improvement: Using Metrics to Your Advantage

In the region of self-improvement, it is regularly stated that "what receives measured gets managed." This profound statement highlights the critical function that information and metrics play in our journey in the direction of private increase. When we follow this precept to conquering self-sabotage, it becomes a powerful device for transformation. In this exploration, we can delve into statistics-pushed self-development, uncovering how monitoring quantitative and qualitative changes allow you to discover and triumph over self-sabotaging behaviors. We'll also test treasured machine and apps that will help you in this transformative device.

Quantitative vs. Qualitative Changes: Balancing the Equation

Before diving into the metrics worldwide, it's miles important to understand the distinction among quantitative and qualitative adjustments. These dimensions of self-improvement may be taken into consideration the "what" and the "how" of your improvement.

Quantitative adjustments involve measurable, numerical records. These are the tangible, concrete metrics that can be tracked over the years. When it involves self-sabotage, quantitative adjustments might probable encompass:

Frequency: How frequently do self-sabotaging behaviors upward thrust up?

Duration: How prolonged do they final when they do arise?

Impact: What is the importance of the damage they cause?

Recovery time: How speedy do you get better from setbacks?

On the other hand, qualitative changes are the lots much less tangible factors of self-improvement. These consist of the nuances of your mind, feelings, and behaviors. Qualitative modifications might also embody the subsequent:

Awareness: How well do you apprehend self-sabotaging thoughts and behaviors?

Emotional well-being: Are you experiencing extra first-rate emotions and much much less terrible ones?

Self-talk: How has your internal talk advanced?

Resilience: How do you control setbacks and demanding conditions?

Balancing each quantitative and qualitative adjustments is critical for holistic self-development. While numerical metrics provide a smooth, aim photo of your development, qualitative adjustments offer insights into the more profound shifts indoors you.

Tools and Apps for Self-Sabotage Measurement

Now that we understand the importance of tracking quantitative and qualitative modifications allow's discover some sensible system and apps which assist you to on your self-sabotage prevention journey. These era are designed to streamline the statistics series device, making monitoring your development lots much less tough.

1.	Self-Reflection Journals: Sometimes, the quality device is a smooth pocket e-book. Regularly jotting down your thoughts, emotions, and behaviors can provide valuable qualitative facts. You can also use it to report the prevalence of self-sabotaging behaviors and your responses to them.

2. Habit-Tracking Apps: Numerous addiction-monitoring apps can help you set dreams, tune your each day conduct, and visualize your improvement. Apps like HabitBull and Habitica let you maintain consistency in your efforts to conquer self-sabotage.

three. Emotion-Tracking Apps: Understanding your emotional patterns is a essential detail of self-development. Apps like MoodTrack and Daylio permit you to log your emotions each day, helping you apprehend triggers for self-sabotaging behaviors.

4. Goal-Setting and Achievement Apps: Apps like Taoist and Trello allow you to in putting clean goals and milestones. They moreover assist you display display screen your improvement in the direction of reaching them, offering quantitative data on your self-improvement journey.

five. Therapeutic Apps: If you choose a more hooked up technique, recuperation apps like CBT Thought Record Diary and Wyse provide cognitive-behavioral strategies and guided wearing sports that will help you combat self-sabotage while monitoring your development.

6. Wellness Wearables: For folks who recognize the combination of generation with each day lifestyles, nicely being wearables like fitness trackers and smartwatches can display display physiological markers which includes coronary heart charge and sleep exquisite, which in a roundabout manner replicate your normal well-being and strain stages.

7. Mindfulness and Meditation Apps: Apps like Headspace and Calm can help you in walking toward mindfulness and meditation, supporting you keep emotional stability and resilience, which may be qualitative markers of self-development.

Embracing Flexibility: Adjusting Your Goals Along the Way

In the pursuit of self-development and the prevention of self-sabotage, putting dreams is a pivotal step. Plans offer us direction, reason, and a experience of fulfillment as we art work in the path of them. However, there may be a touchy stability amongst putting goals and becoming so fixated on them that we inadvertently set ourselves up for failure. This is in which the paintings of embracing flexibility comes into play.

Recognizing When to Pivot

Imagine you're on a street experience, and you've meticulously planned your path. Your vacation spot is marked on the map, and you're determined to conform with that direction with out deviation. But what takes place while you encounter a roadblock, a detour, or an surprising scenic factor of view that beckons you to discover? Do you hold on together together with your inflexible plan or encompass the opportunity to pivot and discover new avenues?

In the adventure of self-improvement, recognizing on the equal time as to pivot is crucial. It's approximately acknowledging that existence is unpredictable and conditions can alternate. Your preliminary goals may also were set primarily based on the records and thoughts-set you had at the begin of your adventure. As you evolve and benefit new reports, your mindset also can moreover shift, predominant you to reevaluate your goals.

Pivoting isn't a sign of failure; it is a signal of adaptability and growth. It technique you are attuned on your internal voice, able to assessing your development, and willing to adjust to live aligned collectively with your values and aspirations. Think of it as recalibrating your compass to navigate the ever-changing panorama of self-development.

Avoiding the Pitfalls of Rigidity

While setting dreams and running toward them is commendable, rigidly adhering to them can cause many troubles. It's vital to renowned that life has sudden traumatic conditions, possibilities, and gaining knowledge of studies. When overly inflexible in pursuing specific objectives, you can inadvertently create an environment ripe for self-sabotage.

1. Burnout: Maintaining an rigid approach can push you to burnout. The regular pressure to meet predefined dreams, regardless of times, can be bodily and mentally tough.

2. Fear of Failure: Rigid dreams can breed a fear of failure. When deviation from the set course is visible as a failure instead of an possibility for increase, it may reason tension and self-doubt.

3. Missed Opportunities: The international is full of surprising possibilities, a number of which may additionally moreover align better along with your evolving values and aspirations. Sticking doggedly on your real plan may possibly purpose you to overlook out on those in all likelihood transformative reviews.

4. Diminished Creativity: Rigidity stifles creativity. It discourages you from wondering out of doors the field and exploring contemporary techniques to self-improvement.

5. Frustration and Discontent: When rigid, setbacks and demanding situations can be intensely disturbing. Instead of seeing them as a part of the gaining knowledge of approach, you may likely view them as roadblocks in your happiness.

It's important to stability having dreams and being bendy for your technique to avoid the ones pitfalls. This ought to now not suggest leaving in the back of your aspirations; it method permitting them to evolve manifestly as you do. Flexibility permits you to conform to converting activities, examine out of your reports, and make knowledgeable options approximately the course of yourself-improvement adventure.

In end, embracing flexibility in aim putting and spotting even as to pivot are essential abilties for stopping self-sabotage. It's a reminder that the adventure of self-improvement is not a at once line but a winding avenue with sudden turns and detours. By staying open to trade and averting the traps of pressure, you may navigate this adventure more effectively and discover it a more fine and enriching experience.

The Power of Self-Reflection: Harnessing the Art of Looking Back

Chapter 13: Creating a Personal Success Journal

A personal success mag is greater than best a diary of your every day sports activities; it's far a dynamic device designed to help you expand and evolve. The gadget begins with deciding on a magazine that resonates with you and invitations you to place your thoughts on paper quite genuinely. This magazine serves as a sacred area wherein you can chronicle your goals, achievements, setbacks, and, most importantly, your journey of self-discovery.

4.   Setting Clear Intentions: Begin your magazine thru placing clean intentions. What do you need to acquire through this workout? Is it to overcome self-sabotage, boom your vanity, or chart your progress towards a specific aim? Having a clear motive in your mag guides your reflections and offers your efforts attention.

five.   Daily Reflections: Dedicate a portion of each day to journaling. Consistency is crucial, whether or not or not or now not within the morning to set intentions for the day or inside the night time to reflect on what transpired. Document your thoughts, feelings, and research without judgment.

6. Goal Tracking: A private achievement mag is an top notch region to music your goals. Write down your brief-term and prolonged-term aspirations, and frequently replace your development. This keeps you accountable and offers a tangible report of your achievements.

Analyzing Past Self-Sabotage Instances for Growth

Now, permit's delve into the coronary heart of self-reflected photograph - studying past self-sabotage instances for growth. Self-sabotage can take many office paintings, from procrastination and self-doubt to horrific self-talk and fear of achievement. To successfully combat the ones behaviors, it is critical to confront them head-on and studies from them.

5.   Identify Self-Sabotaging Patterns: As you evaluation your magazine entries, pay precise interest to moments while you may have sabotaged your improvement. Look for ordinary topics, triggers, and conditions that result in self-sabotage. Were there particular thoughts or emotions that surfaced throughout these times?

6.   Explore the 'Why': Once you have got recognized self-sabotaging patterns, dig deeper to understand the underlying 'why.' What fears, insecurities, or limiting ideals can be using those behaviors? By pinpointing the premise motives, you could start to deal with them correctly.

7.   Seek Alternatives: With insights from your magazine, brainstorm opportunity behaviors and techniques to counter self-sabotage. For instance, when you have a propensity to procrastinate on the identical time as confronted with a daunting mission, discover techniques together with time

control, breaking obligations into smaller steps, or searching for out of doors obligation.

8.   Track Progress: As you placed into impact those alternatives, use your mag to music your development. Note any adjustments for your thoughts, emotions, and behaviors as you figure to triumph over self-sabotage. Celebrate small victories alongside the way, and don't be discouraged with the aid of occasional setbacks.

In give up, the strength of self-mirrored image, via developing a non-public success journal and reading past self-sabotage times for growth, is a transformative adventure of self-discovery and improvement. It's a device that allows you to shine a mild on the shadows indoors, recognize your self more deeply, and ultimately, damage free from self-sabotaging behaviors. Remember that this manner takes time and persistence, but with willpower and perseverance, you could find out yourself on a course to greater self-consciousness and lasting first-rate change.

So, pick up that magazine and begin writing to a higher, extra empowered you.

Setting and Celebrating Milestones: Making Progress Tangible

In the grand tapestry of private development and self-improvement, few subjects are as important as putting and celebrating milestones. These stepping stones pave the manner for lasting alternate, supporting you navigate the often winding avenue of transformation. In this financial disaster, we are going to delve deep into the artwork of putting in location possible checkpoints and the importance of worthwhile your self whilst you hit the ones milestones. By the stop, you could apprehend why milestones depend and the manner to make them be sincerely right for you.

The Significance of Milestones

Before diving into the realistic factors of setting and celebrating milestones, allow's first find out why they'll be so critical in pursuing self-sabotage prevention and private growth.

1. Clarity and Direction: Milestones provide a roadmap for your adventure. They harm down your final intention into smaller, feasible factors, making the path beforehand a good deal much less daunting.

2. Motivation and Momentum: Achieving milestones gives a revel in of fulfillment and a motivational enhance. These small victories can remind you of your development, propelling you forward even as boundaries seem.

3. Accountability: When you put milestones, you create a sense of responsibility. You have tangible goals to fulfill, making assessing your determination and dedication on your desires much less complicated.

four. Measurement of Progress: Milestones act as benchmarks in opposition to which you could degree your improvement. They help you song how a long way you have come and the way near you're to accomplishing your final goal.

Let's explore a way to successfully set and celebrate the ones crucial waypoints in yourself-sabotage prevention journey.

Establishing Achievable Checkpoints

2.	Be Specific

Milestones must be unique and nicely-described. Instead of placing a vague aim like "stop self-sabotaging," destroy it down into measurable additives. For instance, you'll possibly place a milestone like "choose out and replace one self-sabotaging behavior inside the subsequent month."

2.	Make Them Realistic

While ambition is admirable, putting unrealistic milestones can result in frustration and demotivation. Ensure your milestones are possible inside the given time frame and property. Gradual progress is often greater sustainable than trying to perform too much too short.

2.   Set a Timeline

Establish a easy time frame for carrying out every milestone. Having a remaining date creates a experience of urgency and prevents procrastination. It also permits you test whether or no longer you're making suitable enough improvement.

2.   Prioritize and Sequence

Consider the logical series of milestones. Some may also need to be finished earlier than others come to be possible. Prioritize them therefore to ensure a clean development toward your final purpose.

Rewarding Yourself for Hitting Milestones

Setting milestones is only half of of the equation; celebrating them is further vital. Rewards now not most effective broadly identified your achievements however also toughen extraordinary conduct. Here's a way to pass about it:

2.   Choose Meaningful Rewards

Your rewards need to align alongside side your non-public opportunities and values. A tip that is sizeable to you can function a powerful motivator. It may be as smooth as treating your self to a fave meal or taking a break day to lighten up.

2.   Celebrate Sincerely

When you bought a milestone, make the effort to have an wonderful time your accomplishment genuinely. Acknowledge the attempt to dedication it took to get there. Share your achievement with pals or circle of relatives who help your journey.

2.   Reflect and Adjust

After celebrating, take a second to reflect in your improvement and the course in advance. Use this contemplated photo as an opportunity to regulate your desires and milestones as favored. Your journey is dynamic, and adapting alongside the way is ok.

2.   Avoid Self-Criticism

Lastly, avoid the entice of self-complaint if you come upon setbacks or pass over a milestone. Self-improvement is a way, and low stumbles are a part of the adventure. Instead of dwelling on screw ups, reputation on studying and readjusting your approach.

In quit, setting and celebrating milestones is a dynamic and empowering way that could notably decorate yourself-sabotage prevention efforts. By setting up capability checkpoints and profitable yourself for hitting them, you're making development tangible and infuse your journey with motivation and positivity. Remember, each milestone reached is a testomony for your boom and resilience on the direction to self-development. So, set the ones milestones and have fun your adventure toward a higher, extra fulfilled you.

Accountability Partnerships: How Sharing Progress Boosts Success

Have you ever were given down to collect a extensive motive, pleasant to lose motivation and slip lower back into antique behavior alongside the manner? If so, you aren't by me. The journey inside the path of personal increase and self-development may be tough, and it is easy to get derailed by manner of self-doubt or procrastination. This is wherein the idea of responsibility partnerships comes into play. By sharing your development and preserving each particular accountable, you could considerably decorate your opportunities of Success. In this article, we are going to delve into the blessings of responsibility pals and offer techniques for effective check-ins to ensure that your obligation partnership becomes a effective tool in yourself-sabotage prevention toolkit.

Chapter 14: The Benefits of Accountability Buddies

Before we dive into the techniques for powerful check-ins, allows find out why duty partnerships are so effective in boosting Success:

6.   Motivation Amplification: When you have got got have been given an duty associate, you're answerable to yourself and someone else. This delivered layer of responsibility can provide a powerful motivator to stick in your dreams and stay on course.

7.   Increased Commitment: Knowing a person is relying on you can appreciably growth your dedication in your goals. You're a whole lot a whole lot much less probable to hotel to procrastination or self-sabotage whilst someone is based totally in your improvement.

eight. Real-Time Feedback: Accountability partners can provide precious insights and comments to your adventure. They can offer a easy perspective, advocate opportunity strategies, and help you navigate barriers you could no longer have visible.

9. Celebrating Success Together: Achieving desires is greater amusing whilst you may rejoice with a person who is aware of the try you have got established. Sharing your successes together with your obligation partner can inspire and satisfy you.

10. Emotional Support: The adventure of self-improvement can be emotionally taxing at times. Having a person to percentage your highs and lows with can provide emotional guide and assist you live resilient in the face of challenges.

Strategies for Effective Check-Ins

Now that we have were given explored the blessings of obligation partnerships allow's communicate a manner to make your test-ins collectively with your responsibility partner as powerful as possible:

nine. Set Clear Expectations: Define your desires and expectations for the partnership from the outset. What are you each hoping to reap? How regularly will you take a look at in? What techniques of communication will you operate? Clarity is crucial to a successful partnership.

10.   Regular Communication: Consistency is vital. Set a agenda in your check-ins, whether or now not it's miles every day, weekly, or month-to-month. Stick to this time table as cautiously as viable to maintain momentum.

11.   Share development Honestly: Be open and sincere approximately your improvement, even in case you've faced setbacks. Transparency is crucial for responsibility to paintings correctly. If you are suffering, your associate can provide useful aid and guidance.

12.   Set SMART Goals: Ensure that your goals are Specific, Measurable, Achievable, Relevant, and Time-positive (SMART). This makes it much less complex to song

development and offers readability on what Success looks as if.

thirteen. Problem-Solve Together: Use your obligation accomplice as a sounding board while encountering limitations or stressful situations. Brainstorm answers together and adapt your approach as needed.

14. Celebrate Achievements: Don't forget about to have amusing your successes, regardless of how small they'll appear. Acknowledging your development can decorate motivation and keep a first rate outlook.

15. Offer Constructive Feedback: Be supportive and optimistic in your remarks. Avoid judgment or grievance, and hobby on how you can help each exclusive beautify.

sixteen. Adjust as Needed: Life is dynamic, and your desires can also additionally trade. Be open to adjusting your dreams and techniques as your adventure progresses.

In quit, obligation partnerships are a sturdy device for stopping self-sabotage and reaching personal goals. By harnessing the benefits of getting an obligation friend and implementing effective check-in techniques, you can considerably increase your probabilities of Success on your journey of self-development. So, do no longer hesitate to are attempting to find a like-minded accomplice and embark in this transformative journey collectively. Remember, your Success is best a partnership away!

Data-Driven Self-Improvement: Using Metrics to Your Advantage

In the world of self-improvement, it is regularly stated that "what gets measured receives controlled." This profound declaration highlights the vital position that facts and metrics play in our adventure closer to personal boom. When we study this precept to conquering self-sabotage, it becomes a effective tool for transformation. In this exploration, we are going to delve into statistics-pushed self-improvement, uncovering how tracking quantitative and qualitative adjustments permit you to perceive and triumph over self-sabotaging behaviors. We'll furthermore study treasured system and apps to help you on this transformative method.

Quantitative vs. Qualitative Changes: Balancing the Equation

Before diving into the metrics worldwide, it's far vital to apprehend the difference amongst quantitative and qualitative changes. These dimensions of self-improvement may be considered the "what" and the "how" of your improvement.

Quantitative modifications contain measurable, numerical facts. These are the tangible, concrete metrics that may be tracked through the years. When it involves self-sabotage, quantitative adjustments might also include:

Frequency: How often do self-sabotaging behaviors arise?

Duration: How prolonged do they closing once they do stand up?

Impact: What is the fee of the harm they cause?

Recovery time: How brief do you get better from setbacks?

On the alternative hand, qualitative modifications are the lots much much less tangible factors of self-development. These encompass the nuances of your thoughts, feelings, and behaviors. Qualitative adjustments may additionally embody the subsequent:

Awareness: How nicely do you apprehend self-sabotaging mind and behaviors?

Emotional properly-being: Are you experiencing greater powerful feelings and much much less horrible ones?

Self-communicate: How has your inner speak advanced?

Resilience: How do you manage setbacks and challenges?

Balancing each quantitative and qualitative changes is critical for holistic self-improvement. While numerical metrics offer a clean, intention photo of your progress, qualitative adjustments offer insights into the extra profound shifts interior you.

Tools and Apps for Self-Sabotage Measurement

Now that we recognize the significance of monitoring quantitative and qualitative adjustments allow's find out some realistic equipment and apps which can help you on yourself-sabotage prevention adventure. These technology are designed to streamline the statistics collection manner, making monitoring your development a good deal much less hard.

8. Self-Reflection Journals: Sometimes, the first-class device is a easy pocket ebook. Regularly jotting down your thoughts, feelings, and behaviors can offer valuable qualitative statistics. You can also use it to file the prevalence of self-sabotaging behaviors and your responses to them.

nine. Habit-Tracking Apps: Numerous addiction-tracking apps will will will let you set desires, tune your each day habits, and visualize your progress. Apps like HabitBull and Habitica will permit you to preserve consistency for your efforts to conquer self-sabotage.

10. Emotion-Tracking Apps: Understanding your emotional styles is a essential thing of self-development. Apps like MoodTrack and Daylio assist you to log your emotions each day, assisting you find out triggers for self-sabotaging behaviors.

11. Goal-Setting and Achievement Apps: Apps like Taoist and Trello permit you to in setting smooth goals and milestones. They

moreover assist you display your improvement within the direction of attaining them, offering quantitative information on your self-improvement journey.

12.   Therapeutic Apps: If making a decision upon a extra based technique, restoration apps like CBT Thought Record Diary and Wyse provide cognitive-behavioral techniques and guided physical sports to help you combat self-sabotage on the equal time as monitoring your development.

thirteen.   Wellness Wearables: For individuals who respect the integration of technology with daily lifestyles, nicely-being wearables like fitness trackers and smartwatches can show physiological markers which include heart fee and sleep satisfactory, which no longer at once replicate your regular properly-being and pressure tiers.

14.   Mindfulness and Meditation Apps: Apps like Headspace and Calm allow you to in practicing mindfulness and meditation,

helping you maintain emotional balance and resilience, which may be qualitative markers of self-improvement.

Conclusion: Navigating Your Journey with Data

Data becomes your compass inside the quest to conquer self-sabotage and attain lasting self-improvement. It guides you alongside the manner and serves as a deliver of motivation and duty. You benefit beneficial insights into your improvement thru tracking quantitative and qualitative adjustments to your behavior, mind, and feelings. Additionally, the tools and apps available in recent times make this approach more accessible and handy.

Remember that the journey within the course of self-development is specific to each individual, and the metrics you choose to tune ought to align along side your personal goals and values. As you embody facts-driven self-improvement, you will find out the strength of size and the first rate capability for transformation within you. So, armed with your preferred device and a willpower to self-discovery, embark on this data-pushed adventure and watch as you navigate the course toward a self-sabotage-unfastened, thriving destiny.

Embracing Flexibility: Adjusting Your Goals Along the Way

In the pursuit of self-development and the prevention of self-sabotage, putting dreams is a pivotal step. Plans provide us route, purpose, and a enjoy of fulfillment as we paintings in the direction of them. However, there can be a touchy balance among placing desires and turning into so fixated on them that we inadvertently set ourselves up for failure. This is in which the artwork of embracing flexibility comes into play.

Recognizing When to Pivot

Imagine you are on a avenue ride, and you have meticulously deliberate your route. Your tour spot is marked on the map, and you're determined to have a take a look at that direction without deviation. But what happens even as you come across a roadblock, a detour, or a surprising scenic angle that beckons you to find out? Do you preserve on with your inflexible plan or embody the possibility to pivot and find out new avenues?

In the adventure of self-development, recognizing even as to pivot is important. It's about acknowledging that lifestyles are unpredictable and instances can change. Your preliminary dreams may also moreover have been set primarily based totally on the facts and thoughts-set you had on the start of your journey. As you evolve and benefit new stories, your mind-set may additionally additionally shift, important you to reevaluate your objectives.

Pivoting isn't a sign of failure; it's far a sign of adaptability and boom. It way you are attuned on your internal voice, capable of assessing your development, and inclined to adjust to live aligned together together with your values and aspirations. Think of it as recalibrating your compass to navigate the ever-changing panorama of self-improvement.

Avoiding the Pitfalls of Rigidity

While setting goals and running in the direction of them is commendable, rigidly adhering to them can cause many problems. It's crucial to widely known that life has sudden traumatic conditions, possibilities, and learning research. When overly inflexible in pursuing unique desires, you could inadvertently create an environment ripe for self-sabotage.

1. Burnout: Maintaining an rigid approach can push you to burnout. The constant strain to fulfill predefined desires, no matter situations, may be bodily and mentally hard.

2. Fear of Failure: Rigid desires can breed a worry of failure. When deviation from the set course is visible as a failure in preference to

an opportunity for growth, it can reason tension and self-doubt.

3. Missed Opportunities: The worldwide is complete of sudden possibilities, some of which may also moreover align higher together with your evolving values and aspirations. Sticking doggedly to your specific plan may additionally cause you to overlook out on the ones probably transformative critiques.

four. Diminished Creativity: Rigidity stifles creativity. It discourages you from thinking outdoor the field and exploring innovative methods to self-improvement.

five. Frustration and Discontent: When rigid, setbacks and stressful situations can be intensely hectic. Instead of seeing them as part of the gaining knowledge of system, you may view them as roadblocks for your happiness.

It's essential to balance having dreams and being bendy for your technique to avoid those pitfalls. This does now not suggest leaving in the back of your aspirations; it manner allowing them to evolve in reality as you do. Flexibility permits you to conform to converting situations, studies from your evaluations, and make informed selections approximately the route of your self-improvement journey.

In stop, embracing flexibility in reason putting and spotting whilst to pivot are essential competencies for preventing self-sabotage. It's a reminder that the journey of self-improvement isn't always a right now line however a winding road with surprising turns and detours. By staying open to exchange and retaining off the traps of pressure, you may navigate this journey more successfully and find out it a greater pleasing and enriching enjoy.

Chapter 15: Mindful Self-Assessment

In the hustle and bustle of our speedy-paced lives, getting caught up within the whirlwind of ordinary pastime is just too clean. We regularly find out ourselves racing in the direction of our goals, craving for self-development, and striving to interrupt unfastened from self-sabotaging behavior. While ambition and strain are surely commendable trends, the course to personal boom is often obscured with the resource of the fog of assessment and the relentless pursuit of day after today's achievements. During the ones moments, the concept of aware self-assessment comes into play.

Practicing Mindfulness to Evaluate Progress

Mindfulness, a exercise rooted in ancient facts, has gained incredible recognition in latest years for its transformative consequences on mental nicely-being and private development. At its center, mindfulness is ready being surely present in the 2nd, with an open and non-judgmental focus of our thoughts, emotions, and surroundings. Yet, its utility extends past stress good buy and emotional regulation; it could additionally be a potent device for assessing and improving our improvement towards self-development.

But how can mindfulness help us in comparing our adventure toward overcoming self-sabotage? The solution lies in its functionality to foster heightened self-recognition and a deeper reference to our inner selves.

When we exercise mindfulness within the context of self-evaluation, we start by means of way of looking our mind and behaviors with out casting judgment. This independent self-statement permits us to benefit insights into our types of self-sabotage, triggers, and emotional responses. It lets in us to step once more from the constant pressure for progress and, rather, cognizance at the exceptional of our adventure.

Here are some realistic steps to include aware self-evaluation into your lifestyles:

1.	Daily Mindfulness Practice: Dedicate time each day to mindfulness meditation or truely being found for your each day sports activities. During those moments, have a observe your mind, feelings, and actions without in search of to exchange or choose them.

2.	Journaling: Maintain a mindfulness journal in that you record your observations. This can encompass noting times of self-sabotage, triggers, and your emotional united states on the time.

3.	Regular Self-Check-Ins: Throughout the day, pause to check in with yourself. Ask questions like, "How am I feeling proper now?" or "What thoughts are dominating my mind?" This exercising let you stay grounded and conscious.

four. Mindful Breathing: Whenever you word strain, anxiety, or self-doubt creeping in, take a few aware breaths. Inhale intensely, recognition for your breath, and exhale slowly, releasing anxiety.

5.   Non-Judgmental Self-Reflection: When evaluating your improvement, keep away from harsh self-grievance. Instead, approach your observations with kindness and interest, like a compassionate buddy presenting manual.

Avoiding the Comparison Trap

One of the pitfalls that may derail our journey to self-improvement is the insidious entice of evaluation. In an age of social media, it is clean to evaluate our improvement, successes and struggles to those of others. This constant publicity to the spotlight reels of diverse people's lives can foster feelings of inadequacy and self-doubt, important to a poisonous cycle of self-sabotage.

Mindful self-assessment encourages us to break free from this evaluation lure via redirecting our interest inward. When we're absolutely present in our very personal studies, we recognize that our journey is uniquely our private, and comparing it to someone else's direction isn't always sincere or inexperienced.

Here are some techniques to keep away from the evaluation trap:

1.   Limit Social Media: Consider lowering your exposure to social media systems that cause assessment. Unfollow money owed that make you sense inadequate and curate your feed to encompass first-rate and galvanizing content fabric material.

2.   Practice Gratitude: Regularly remind your self of your accomplishments and development. Gratitude in your adventure can assist shift your attention away from what others are doing.

three. Celebrate Small Wins: Acknowledge and feature fun your milestones, regardless of how minor they'll seem. These are your victories in your specific route.

four. Seek Supportive Communities: Surround your self with people who uplift and inspire you in desire to fueling the evaluation recreation. Join groups or corporations that percentage your dreams and values.

5.   Embrace Self-Compassion: Treat your self with the identical kindness and compassion you'll provide to a pal managing comparable stressful situations. Remember that everyone has their struggles and setbacks.

In quit, conscious self-assessment is a powerful device that lets in us to stay located in our journey toward self-improvement. By training mindfulness, we benefit deeper insights into our development and forms of self-sabotage. Furthermore, via the usage of warding off the assessment trap, we're able to make certain that our journey stays uniquely our very own, free from the distractions and pitfalls of out of doors comparisons. So, as you navigate the direction to non-public increase, endure in thoughts to be type to your self, live present, and encompass the knowledge of conscious self-assessment.

Feedback and Self-Improvement: Constructive Criticism as a Catalyst

At the coronary heart of private growth and self-development lies a vital fact: the potential to are in search of for and encompass feedback is one of the maximum powerful equipment for your arsenal. Yet, for plenty, the mere component out of grievance can evoke apprehension and vulnerability. We regularly partner feedback with judgment, viewing it through a lens of negativity. However, in self-sabotage prevention and personal development, feedback isn't always your enemy; it is your exceptional friend, your catalyst for boom. In this exploration of "Feedback and Self-Improvement," we are capable of delve into looking for comments from depended on property and learning the alchemy of turning criticism into opportunities for transformation.

Seeking Feedback from Trusted Sources

The journey to self-development and self-sabotage prevention is profoundly private, however it want not be a solitary enterprise. Seeking remarks from relied on assets can provide useful insights and perspectives you can not in any other case discover. Here's the way to navigate this crucial problem of your adventure:

1.   Identify Your Trusted Circle: Start by means of way of identifying people for your life who absolutely care about your nicely-being and growth. These can be near buddies, family individuals, mentors, or colleagues who understand your desires and function your great hobbies at coronary coronary coronary heart.

2.   Clear Communication: Approach your trusted property with a clean intention. Let them recognize you rate their critiques and actively are trying to find their enter as a part of your self-development journey.

Transparency can set the level for optimistic remarks.

three. Ask the Right Questions: Be precise approximately what you want at the equal time as soliciting comments. Are you searching out input on a specific thing of your behavior, communication, or abilties? Frame your questions in a manner that invites considerate responses.

4. Active Listening: As you get hold of comments, exercise lively listening. This method in fact absorbing what your trusted resources are announcing with out right now getting shielding or dismissive. Remember, feedback is a present, no matter the reality that wrapped in critique.

5. Balanced Perspective: Don't depend mostly on one supply for feedback. Collect input from multiple relied on people to benefit a more balanced and entire information of your strengths and areas for improvement.

Turning Criticism into Opportunities for Growth

Now, permit's address the artwork of turning criticism into opportunities for growth. Complaints, despite the fact that brought constructively, can be tough to digest. However, studying this ability is vital to stopping self-sabotage and fostering private development:

1.   Embrace a Growth Mindset: Criticism is not a judgment of your nicely worth but an evaluation of your moves or behavior. Adopt a boom mind-set that views challenges and setbacks as possibilities to analyze and evolve.

2.   Detach Emotionally: It's natural to have an emotional reaction to grievance. Allow yourself to feel those emotions, but do now not allow them to cloud your judgment. Step decrease back and objectively examine the remarks.

9 781999 156435